Two . . . Becoming One *provides a blueprint for marriage. It has revolutionized our marriage. I believe your marriage will be blessed if you read and apply the faith concepts found in this book.*

Joe Gibbs
President, Joe Gibbs Racing
Former head coach, three-time Super Bowl
champion Washington Redskins

Is it realistic? Is it scriptural? Is it balanced? Is it believable? Two . . . Becoming One *combines all four ingredients. This is an honest book with practical content.*

Charles Swindoll
President of Dallas Theological Seminary
Speaker, Insight for Living radio program

If I had it within my power, Two . . . Becoming One *would be required reading for every couple.*

Dennis Rainey
President of Family life Ministry,
Host of Family Life Today radio programs

Don and Sally Meredith are two of God's choicest servants and longtime friends. This book is must reading for all who desire to experience a rich and God-blessed marriage.

Bill Bright
Founder and President,
Campus Crusade for Christ

Don and Sally Meredith apply sound, biblical wisdom to the tough issues of marriage—communication, how to grow in oneness, finances, facing trials, romance, and sorting out the biblical roles of husbands and wives. This material is so good that Christian Financial Concepts will include it in our new Resourceful Living Series curriculum.

Larry Burkett
Founder and CEO
Christian Financial Concepts

Two... Becoming One

Experiencing the Power of Oneness in Your Marriage

DON AND **SALLY MEREDITH**

MOODY PRESS
CHICAGO

Printed in the United States of America

to our children
who have blessed our lives incredibly
and now have become our best friends:

Todd and Sara Meredith
Scott and Carmen Gertz
Kathryn Meredith
Brad and Tiffany Haines

Contents

Foreword

*P*at and I have been married for over thirty years now. We're both professing Christians, and we actively seek God's direction in our lives. But I'll be the first to admit that I'm not always the world's best husband. Pat can readily attest to this. And she'd tell you that she's not always the perfect wife. We try, but though we deeply love each other, we sometimes fail.

I'll level with you: Sometimes I used to put my career as an NFL football coach above everything, occasionally even God! And the pressures of running our NASCAR team have made me difficult to be around at times. As for Pat, every now and then her frustration in defining her role, now that our kids have grown up, surfaces. Yet, there was the time when she faced a serious, life-threatening illness and her faith never wavered. I love her for the way she responded to God.

Through it all, we believe that God made our marriage, and that He has a plan for it. That's why we strongly recommend, and practice, the marriage principles that Don and Sally lay out in *Two . . . Becoming One.*

This book provides a biblical blueprint for marriage. Don and Sally show God's commitment to marriage and our responsibility to Him and each other. They call this commitment a "faith relationship," and it has revolutionized our marriage. God does have a plan and practical solutions for your marriage, whether you are happily married, have hit some painful trials, or wonder if you're married to someone you believe is not God's best for you. Whatever your situation, *Two . . . Becoming One* will set you straight. It will give you biblical hope and direction.

Don and Sally are dear friends, and our families are very close. We've spent enough time together to know that they use these principles in their own marriage. So do our married children. Pat and I, our son J. D. and his wife, Melissa, took the twelve-week *Becoming One* course. We highly recommend the *Two . . . Becoming One Workbook,* based on that course, after you finish this book.

This material has blessed thousands of marriages. The material presented in this book is the foundation for two fine ministries: Christian Family Life, which focuses on marital counseling and small groups, and the Family Life Ministry of Campus Crusade, which holds the tremendous weekend marriage conferences.

I believe your marriage will be blessed if you read and apply the faith concepts described in *Two . . . Becoming One.* It has blessed our lives and those of our children. We will forever be grateful to the Merediths for sharing the faith-relationship concept with us.

JOE GIBBS
President, Joe Gibbs Racing
Former head coach, three-time Super Bowl
champion Washington Redskins

Acknowledgments

*S*ally and I are very aware of the individuals and groups who have influenced our lives and this book over the years. We know that the Holy Spirit has used each one of these friends to contribute insights to this message. We are very thankful for each person.

Howard Hendricks, professor emeritus of Dallas Theological Seminary, has greatly impacted the development of this book. During my (Don's) years of study under him, I learned valuable lessons and received great encouragement.

Two groups have been equally important to us. First, we owe significant gratitude to the original founders of Christian Family Life. Many of the insights in this book are directly attributable to them. We are especially grateful to Dr. Barry Leventhal, our faithful friend, who has always taken time to help us biblically. We are also thankful to Dennis Rainey and the Family Life Ministry staff of Campus Crusade for Christ and particularly grateful that they teach these faith concepts at their seminars.

Over the years, numerous good friends have contributed individual help in typing and editing. Others have contributed over the last thirty-five years through their financial and prayer support for our ministry. We owe a debt of gratitude to each of you.

We want to thank Mike Taylor for the hours he spent editing the earlier version. He has improved the text greatly. Our thanks also to Jim Bell Jr. and Jim Vincent of Moody Press for their gracious help and encouragement. Your contributions are greatly appreciated. And finally, thanks to Sam Conway for introducing us to the Moody Press team.

PART ONE

Why Marriages Fail

ONE

"But Sally, It's Third and Eight!"

Do you know a couple with a great marriage, one so solid that you would trade your marriage for theirs? Probably not. Most counselors that we have known agree that the majority of marriages today are either hurting badly or are on the verge of breaking up. Marriages are failing in tremendous numbers.

All things considered, marriage today is a risky proposition. In recent times, applications for divorce number about the same as applications for marriage licenses in most major U.S. cities. "In 1990, there were forty-eight divorces for each one-hundred marriages," reported researcher George Barna.[1] In the nineties there has been one divorce for every 1.8 marriages. Divorce cases affect more than one million children each year, and "13 million children under eighteen have one or both parents missing."[2] As alarming as those figures are, additional research reveals that many marriages not visited by divorce are hurting; the parents are attempting to "hang in there" for the sake of the children.

Is the situation hopeless? No. Not only is marriage as an institution not hopeless, it can succeed beyond one's expectations. The successful marriage, though, begins with an attitude and a dedication: *Happy marriages are made, not found.* Begin now to earnestly seek the answers on how to succeed in marriage. Both married couples and those planning to marry must recognize that romantic feelings or good intentions are not enough. Couples must work to strengthen marriages. The good news is: God designed marriage, so He can make it work!

Before we look at God's plan for making marriage work, let us introduce ourselves and look at how marriages begin to deteriorate (the focus of part 1). Sally and I have been married more than thirty years, and we continue to be amazed by the love and satisfaction we feel for each other. Even though we are just human beings with strengths and weaknesses, God has shown us the key to loving by faith. As our faith has grown, God has given us the ability to love with a love that honors and gives hope to the other.

Each of us has weaknesses, as do all husbands and wives. Sally's shortcomings used to really bother me, and mine upset her too. But we now see our weaknesses in a realistic way, and we experience an exhilarating love for each other. That's a miracle. It hasn't always been that way. In 1967, when we married, such love was foreign to us. At that time our love was based on performance. And unfortunately, we each began to fall short of the other's expectations beginning on our wedding day.

MY FOOTBALL BRIDE
(Don's Story)

After a three-month engagement, our wedding day arrived. Because we were both twenty-seven and had been Christians longer than most newlyweds, we thought marriage would be a little bit easier for us. Frankly, we were naïve and overconfident. We struggled from the very first day.

Our different backgrounds surfaced on the day of the wedding. The ceremony was scheduled at 4:00 on a Saturday afternoon in the early fall. Since I (Don) was ahead of schedule, I flipped on the television to catch the first University of Texas football game of the season. I hadn't seen a game in six months. Before I knew it, it was 3:45

and I wasn't completely ready. Frustrated that I had to leave the game before halftime, I rushed off to the wedding. Go ahead and chastise me, women. I realize that I deserve it.

After the ceremony in Boulder, Colorado, we left for Vail, where we had reservations in a lovely hotel. As soon as we pulled out of the church parking lot, I quickly switched on the radio, trying to catch the end of the Texas game. The experts said 1967 would be the "year of the Horns" (Texas Longhorns). I just had to know the score!

No luck. The mountains limited the radio reception, throwing me into a "sports panic." I decided to stop short of Vail and find another motel just so I wouldn't miss the 10:00 news and the Texas score. To me, one hotel was as good as another. When I suggested that we stop early, Sally thought I was anxious for the honeymoon night. Well, I was. But the Texas score, now *that* was a really important issue! Mind you, I didn't intend to hurt Sally with my fixation on Texas football. Why, I was behaving like any red-blooded, twenty-seven-year-old Texan would! Unfortunately, I was giving first place to football over my new bride. This wasn't the first or the last time I did this.

We stopped forty miles east of Vail, checked into a motel, had dinner, and got back to the room about 10:15—just in time for the sports report. My adrenaline was pumping—to discover the Texas football score. As my bride disappeared into the bathroom to prepare for our wedding night, I quickly clicked on the television and learned the big news of the day: *Texas had been defeated.* I was literally sick! I can still remember trying to regain my composure as Sally entered the room. She had no idea how important football was in my life, and how upset I was by the opening-day Texas tragedy. Of course, I had never communicated any of this to her.

The very next day brought more conflicts. That morning, on our first full day of married life, we drove on to Vail. Sally had envisioned us spending time together by hiking in the mountains—a romantic outdoors-type honeymoon in the breathtaking mountains of Colorado. But after two hours of walking around gazing at trees, my mind began drifting to thoughts of the NFL, completed passes, and touchdowns. *After all,* I told myself, *when you've seen one tree, you've seen them all.* Wouldn't you know, the Dallas Cowboys and the Green Bay Packers were scheduled to play that afternoon!

Feeling perfectly justified and believing that Sally wanted to watch football also, I began speeding toward Denver in order to find a hotel—and a television with the big game. I knew if we stopped for lunch, we'd miss the start of the game. So we bought some cheese and crackers at a country store and headed for Denver. Of course, I got a speeding ticket along the way. By this time Sally was a very disappointed bride. She sat in silence in the car. No problem; I just figured she didn't have anything to say.

When we arrived in Denver, I suggested that we buy some Kentucky Fried Chicken and take it to the room. She bought a magazine to read while I watched the game. To my dismay, she wasn't very excited about all the big plays. It dawned on me that Sally knew nothing about football when she commented, "Hey, that guy has the same name as you," speaking of the all-pro Dallas Cowboy quarterback, Don Meredith. I remember looking at her and saying, "You've got to be kidding. Do you know anything about football?" to which she replied, "I could care less." Wouldn't you know, the Cowboys lost that day, and I was sick again!

From Sally's viewpoint, the honeymoon (perhaps even the marriage) was a total disaster. The discussion we had that night was mild compared to the ones we had throughout the rest of the football season. Every Saturday and Sunday I could be found sitting in front of the tube watching football games.

Sally actually had nothing against football; she had just never thought much about it. Her idea of a pleasant autumn day was walking or riding through the woods, enjoying the changing colors of trees and smelling the brisk autumn air. Again, I thought, *Trees are trees. What's the big deal about trees?*

Already seeds of conflict were beginning to germinate in our marriage. Now, neither of us was right or wrong; well, maybe I was a bit entranced—obsessed?—with football, but my desire to be with Sally was no less. We both meant well; we didn't want to hurt each other. But we did! Clearly our differing backgrounds were beginning to collide and damage our relationship.

Another discouraging force was *our tendency to focus on performance.* We began to notice every failure and weakness in each other. It became absurd. For example, Sally was a good housekeeper, but if she didn't do one particular thing like my mother had, I became critical and drilled her about that one point. I was mature enough to know better, but I couldn't seem to help my critical attitude. She, on the other hand, would criticize the fact that I read the sports page the first thing each morning instead of the Bible. She wanted a "spiritual leader," but all I could think about was football!

Several things stood out. I was amazed at how my feelings of love for her could change so quickly when I was hurt. A jolted marriage relationship can be intensely painful. Rejection, insults, insecurities, and lost devotion can ravage one's emotions. I found that after being wounded emotionally, my strongest feelings of love could quickly change to bitterness.

In spite of our good intentions, we began to find it hard to live together. I can remember thinking to myself that I just couldn't let things continue in the direction they were going. But they did. In just two years, our very best intentions for a model Christian marriage had become, at best, a memory of the past. Things were just mediocre.

The purpose of this book is to help couples avoid ever reaching this unfortunate and unnecessary point in marriage. Tragically, most couples naïvely feel this sort of situation will never happen to them. "We are different. We love each other so much!" they say.

By God's grace, our marriage did not remain mired in mediocrity. During our third year of marriage, while we were involved in a college campus ministry, I noticed that a number of students were getting involved in foolish dating relationships. I saw a need for someone to teach the students some biblical guidelines for dating. So I began to page through the Bible to discover those key insights. It was during this study of dating and marriage that Sally and I discovered our own need.

God changed our marriage. Perhaps those students don't remember much of what we said, but for the Merediths, marriage has never been the same.

TRANSFORMING TRUTHS

The rest of this book is our attempt to describe the biblical truths that transformed our marriage. We've seen the same principles work for countless other couples as well. Believe me, our improvement has not been based on personal strengths. These discoveries stand on the certainty of the Scriptures and God's statement that He intends for marriage to be a blessing. That call for people to bless each other was stated by Peter to the New Testament church, and it certainly applies to the relationship between Christian husbands and wives: "To sum up, all of you be harmonious, sympathetic, brotherly, kindhearted, and humble in spirit; not returning evil for evil or insult for insult, but giving a blessing instead; for you were called for the very purpose that you might inherit a blessing" (1 Peter 3:8–9).

The first step in solving a problem is to recognize what causes it. For this reason, part 1 of this book attempts to answer the question, "Why are so many marriages failing?" We will discuss six major reasons marriages disintegrate and trace what happens if the causes are not confronted and corrected. Allow me one old football saying: "The best defense is a good offense." If you understand how to recognize and respond to these six factors, you will be much better prepared to thrive in your marriage.

Part 2 describes the spiritual insight necessary to make lasting commitments and changes in marriage. God's purpose for creating marriage will be evident as partners understand His creation plan. This plan can help empower you to experience permanent and fulfilling love. Questions like these will be answered:

- What is God's blueprint for marriage?

- What is love and how can I experience it?

- Did He design my mate for me? If so, why are we struggling so much?

- What part does the Holy Spirit play in marriage?

- What qualities in my life are necessary for me to be a loving spouse?

- How do the roles of the husband and wife work in harmony?

Part 3 gives directions on *how to apply these biblical patterns* to everyday married life. This section *integrates the spiritual and practical sides of marriage.* Questions like these will be covered:

- In what ways do men and women differ? How do these differences create conflict?

- How can your sexual expression grow?

- What should be your perspective on trials?

- How can you overcome in-law problems?

- How can you transform financial issues from dividing your marriage to becoming a source of unity?

Couples who understand why marriages fail as well as how God intends marriage to work have a significant advantage. They are well on the road to a growing and thriving marriage. *God not only designed marriage, He can make it work!*

NOTES

1. George Barna, *The Future of the American Family* (Chicago: Moody, 1993), 67–68.
2. Armand Nicholi Jr., in George A. Rekers, ed., *Family Building* (Ventura, Calif.: Gospel Light, 1985), as cited in Bill Bright, *The Coming Revival* (Orlando: New Life, 1994), 54.

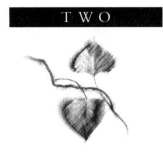

Six Reasons
Marriages Fail

*W*hat stands between you and divorce? Most couples confidently reply:

- "Our love is more mature than most other couples."
- "We are wiser."
- "We are better educated."
- "We have been Christians longer."
- "We know each other so well."

Even though all of those factors will help marriages, they cannot ensure success in marriage. Good intentions will not divorce-proof your marriage. After all, no one gets married expecting the marriage to self-destruct. Yet 50 percent of all divorces occur within three years of saying "I do."[1] Remarkable, isn't it? From "I do" to "Get out!" in less than three years! Among couples who remain married, countless thousands suffer in icy silence, needs unmet, and complete discouragement —a far cry from the joy that God intends for marriage.

So why *do* marriages fail? This chapter will alert you to the six most common reasons that marriages break up. During more than two decades of counseling literally thousands of couples, Sally and I have seen these six tearing away at marriages and often destroying them. All six reasons represent powerful forces; left unchecked, they will silently undermine your most valued human relationship.

We challenge you to learn what these powerful forces are, how to safeguard your marriage, and spread your new insights to extended family and friends. Interestingly, the more confident that couples are concerning their love and commitment, the more closed-minded they are to help or suggestion. The apostle Paul wrote, "Therefore let him who thinks he stands take heed that he does not fall" (1 Corinthians 10:12). Jesus exhorted His followers to count the cost prior to undertaking a significant life commitment. "For which one of you, when he wants to build a tower, does not first sit down and calculate the cost to see if he has enough to complete it? Otherwise, when he has laid a foundation and is not able to finish, all who observe it begin to ridicule him, saying, 'This man began to build and was not able to finish'" (Luke 14:28–30).

Most people complete twelve to sixteen years of schooling to learn a career. But few ever take a course on marriage. No wonder marriages fail—people are not prepared for the most important relationship on this earth.

Have you counted the cost for a successful marriage? Are you prepared to overcome the six most common reasons marriages fail?

REASON ONE:
Differing Backgrounds, Homes, and Environments

Our melting-pot society results in many couples getting married with very different backgrounds. These cultural and family differences often result in immediate disagreements, which lead to conflict and hurt. At first, couples find that it's fun making up. As the differences become more personal and numerous, however, couples begin to focus on the performance of their mate. Over time, this progression begins to undermine their commitment to each other. These differences may touch every activity or belief of the couple.

Early in our marriage, Sally and I had to face adjustments due to family differences. We married after a short engagement, only to discover we really did not know each other very well. Remember, women, as you read this, please do not give up on me! I really didn't intend to hurt Sally.

I grew up in Texas where my parents were outgoing people of modest means. Because Dad was in sales, we were often involved in community-wide social events. We did not have a great deal of money, but I was fairly free financially. Sally, on the other hand, grew up in the mountains of Colorado. Her family had close friends and relatives, but weren't active in social circles. In addition, she was very different in the way she approached finances. I felt considerably freer about spending money, while she was more conservative in her money management.

When my family took vacations, we usually got up early in the morning and drove all day. We stopped at new motels that were certain to be clean and comfortable. We were the "no-surprises" people. Thirty years ago, Holiday Inn fit the bill perfectly. We seldom stopped to eat at expensive restaurants, preferring burgers and fries instead. When we traveled, we were very goal oriented. The vacation started after we arrived at our destination.

By contrast, Sally's family considered the drive as part of the vacation. Since they enjoyed eating out, they splurged on good meals. To afford that, they economized in other areas, primarily in their choice of motels. They shopped motels to find the best deal. I've learned since that many people do that, but at the time it was a real jolt to my country-club pride. Sally always seemed to head for those old, beige-colored stucco motels—you know, the kind with the creaky furniture, the 1926 chenille bedspreads, and the everyday low prices.

The first two days of our honeymoon we stayed in what I considered nice motels. On the third day, we headed for Tulsa. To Sally's great disappointment, I had decided to cut the honeymoon short. After all, there were no more football games, and who wants to look at the trees? Being a Holiday Inn man, I kept driving trying to find one. I wasn't about to lower my standards. It didn't occur to me that in that sparsely populated area of the country, there might not be a Holiday Inn. And since we were still ignorant of each other's choices, Sally couldn't understand why I wouldn't stop. She fell asleep in the car. After driving through town after town with no Holiday Inn, we found ourselves nearly out of gas at two o'clock in the morning. Fortunately, we were close to a small New Mexico town, one hundred miles from nowhere.

There were only three motels in town. To me, they were all the old, unpredictable kind that didn't appeal to my senses at all. To Sally there was nothing unacceptable about them. In fact, she encouraged me to check each motel at 2:00 A.M. for rates! Much to my discomfort, we had to stay, since no gas stations were open at that time of the morning. I lay awake thinking bugs were going to eat me while Sally slept like a baby.

Throughout our travels later that fall, there were many opportunities to stay in motels. Sally, motivated to be a good steward of God's money, just didn't feel right about paying Holiday Inn prices. I didn't want to settle for anything less. Note that it wasn't so much an issue of right or wrong, but of two people with different perspectives. That first year, we experienced some real hurt and conflict over such differences. Because of my strong logical reasoning, I was able to maneuver her toward my thinking, but in the process I unknowingly destroyed some of her respect for me.

It's likely you have married . . . someone very

different from yourself. These differences . . . can lead your

spouse and you down the road to hurt and rejection.

Another example of a difference that caused almost immediate struggle involved our intellectual pursuits. As someone interested in sports activities more than reading, I almost never read a book. I was a *Cliffs Notes* man. I don't think I had read ten books in my entire life up to that point. My bride, on the other hand, was the intellectual in our family. Indeed, she still is an excellent student who loves to read. She came from a family who read constantly.

Later we discovered another difference: Sally is more group-oriented while I am a one-on-one person.

We have since learned to value our differences and learn from one another. I now enjoy reading and even writing, while she has learned to enjoy various sports activities with me. But in those early days, our divergent intellectual and social pursuits were a real problem. We simply placed different values on different things.

When people get married, they're usually at the peak of emotional love. Their intentions are so good, they would do anything for the other. Yet, immediately after the wedding day, they begin to recognize many differences. The examples mentioned above, differences in lodging preferences and in intellectual and social pursuits, may seem small by themselves. But if multiplied by ten other issues, the couple can quickly become overwhelmed with obstacles.

In our diversified American society, it's likely you have married (or will marry) someone very different from yourself. These differences, if not properly anticipated, can lead your spouse and you down the road to hurt and rejection. And for many couples, there's the added emotional baggage from a previous marriage. If stepchildren are also involved, the blending process often can take years to work through.

REASON TWO:
The Deceptive "Fifty-Fifty" Relationship

Marriage, many believe, is a "fifty-fifty" relationship. That belief sounds good and seems to make sense. There's just one problem—*it doesn't work.*

That proposition is the second major reason marriages fail. Here's why: Thinking our spouse must do his or her 50 percent leads us to focus on the other person's performance. Over time, each mate wants to insure that the *other* does *his or her* part. Human nature demands it. Unfortunately, there is no way to know who met whom halfway. It is impossible to know if the other mate cared as much, worked as hard, or felt as strongly. Ultimately, couples are drawn into deeper levels of examination and criticism. Furthermore, the fifty-

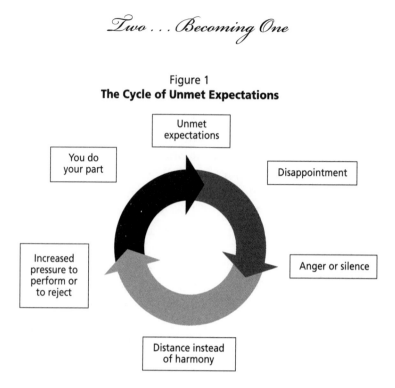

Figure 1
The Cycle of Unmet Expectations

fifty concept actually promotes independence: "You do your part; I'll do mine."

Once couples start measuring each other's performance, *disappointment* follows close behind, leading to feelings of rejection and hurt. Some mates react with anger; others respond with a deafening silence. Either way, a cycle begins (above) resulting in distance.

The resulting frustration reveals the fallacy of the fifty-fifty notion. *It is impossible to believe that the other person has actually met you halfway.* The minute one mate believes the other is not meeting him halfway, condemnation and conflict usually follow.

As newlyweds, Dave and Ruth experienced the cycle above. They became so tense and uptight that they regularly overstated things and made hurtful accusations, such as "Well, maybe we shouldn't have gotten married," or "Maybe I'm not the person you thought I was!" As the arguments escalated, Ruth resorted to cutting remarks, only to have David retaliate. Eventually, Ruth would start crying, march to the bedroom, and slam the door shut. At that, David would get in the car and drive around town, his stomach in a knot.

After an hour or so, he'd return home in hopes of making up to Ruth.

Early in the marriage, they actually enjoyed the making-up scenes, believing them to be evidences of a growing maturity and ability to handle differences. But with the passing of time, the fun of making up faded and their resentment began to slowly build. *If David knew how badly I was hurting, he'd stop yelling at me,* she thought to herself. *He doesn't understand how hurt I am.* Strangely, David had similar thoughts. He could never believe that Ruth cared as much as he did. And he felt he was always the first to give in. Resentment and hostility continued to smolder in each partner, making it more difficult to say, "I'm sorry" and really mean it.

With the cycle in full gear, resentment soon led to anger. David began keeping a mental tally on how Ruth responded. She kept her own score. He studied her every move, looking for an opportunity to criticize. If she didn't respond "properly," that is, *according to David's standard of performance,* he pounced on her mistake. Ruth withdrew into a protective shell of silence.

Maybe you're thinking, "Christians shouldn't have those kind of problems." No, they shouldn't, but, believe us, they do. We find very little difference between Christian and non-Christian couples in our counseling. Entering marriage naïvely, planning to only meet your mate halfway, will guarantee the same results as David and Ruth experienced: bitter frustration and aloneness. The fifty-fifty relationship may work in other areas of life, but it miserably fails in marriage. God has an infinitely better plan!

REASON THREE:
Selfishness

The third reason most marriages fail is outright selfishness. The natural human way is to look out for number one first. The Bible tells us that every person has an inborn sense of selfishness that is capable of incredible devastation. "The heart is more deceitful than all else and is desperately sick; who can understand it?" (Jeremiah 17:9). We don't really believe that about our own hearts, do we? Yet strong, self-centered agendas appear in most marriages, and the mate almost always resists and retaliates against the agenda.

If you aren't yet married or are newly married, you're probably thinking, *That doesn't describe my mate*, or *That's too strong*. Most couples naïvely enter marriage believing their mates are incapable of such actions. But the failure to deal openly with this human tendency frequently leads to disappointment and dissatisfaction in marriage.

The Bible says we all have this innate tendency to look out for ourselves first, and calls it *the flesh, old man,* and *old nature*. It also calls it *sin*. For that reason, only Jesus Christ is able to break this bondage to self and give us a supernatural, divine nature. But even after becoming Christians, we need to mature in the Spirit to rise above selfishness.

You may think you're right; *indeed, perhaps you are.*
But the Lord Jesus calls us to serve one another,

[to put] the well-being of our mate first.

There will be times in marriage when you really want your way. You may think you're right; *indeed, perhaps you are*. But the Lord Jesus calls us to serve one another, and that specifically means putting the well-being of our mate first.

Couples who marry without a firm commitment to sacrifice selfish rights in order to serve the other will invariably inflict emotional pain on one another. Two people with sinful natures who marry don't make for greater peace; rather, great strife and destruction follow.

During counseling, we typically hear statements like, "He doesn't understand me anymore" or "I thought she was a Christian. How can she act that way?" With eyes welling up in tears, some women say, "I can't repeat the words he called me." Some altercations become physically violent with punches thrown and threats to kill. But not everyone is outwardly aggressive. Some seethe in silence, resolving to get even. Christians marry with the best of intentions, only to discover that their lifelong mates are capable of inflicting great hurt, often with little remorse. Feelings of love are replaced with fear. Romance sours. Hostile environments mushroom like ominous summer thunderstorms, reinforcing the tendency to serve oneself first.

Everyone has a choice to make: We can be either a mirror that reflects approval, appreciation, and encouragement to our mates, or we can reflect failure and disappointment. What does your mate get from you? If your reflection is negative, the result will be fear and retaliation. Over time, feelings will become frozen and attitudes critical. And our harsh words and attitudes can be destructive: "'The poison of asps is under their lips; whose mouth is full of cursing and bitterness; their feet are swift to shed blood, destruction and misery are in their paths, and the path of peace they have not known'" (Romans 3:13–17).

Strong words, right? But turn on the nightly news and listen to the description of family life in America. How can one spouse come to the point of killing the one he once loved? *Every family tragedy mentioned above started with good intentions.* The root cause is nothing less than sinful, selfish behavior, and only Christ can deliver. The apostle Paul described the struggle—and the solution—in Romans 7:22–8:2:

> For I joyfully concur with the law of God in the inner man, but I see a different law in the members of my body, waging war against the law of my mind and making me a prisoner of the law of sin which is in my members. Wretched man that I am! Who will set me free from the body of this death? Thanks be to God through Jesus Christ our Lord! So then, on the one hand I myself with my mind am serving the law of God, but on the other, with my flesh the law of sin. Therefor there is now no condemnation for those who are in Christ Jesus. For the law of the Spirit of life in Christ Jesus has set you free from the law of sin and of death.

So take heart. The balance of this book reveals God's plan for a successful, lasting, and joyful marriage. We will see that a successful marriage depends on the Holy Spirit freeing us from our selfish, sinful attitudes.

REASON FOUR:
Inability to Cope with Life's Trials

I used to believe that successful Christians dodged trials like soldiers running through a field of land mines. The people who missed the most mines were successful. Trials were for the unfortunate or unfaithful. As a result, when I married Sally, I had given no thought to facing trials. Although I knew there would be tough times, I expected them to be few and momentary. Most couples marry with a similar perspective, particularly younger newlyweds. We're no longer surprised to hear, "If I had known then what I know now, I would have never gotten married."

This inability to anticipate or cope with the normal trials of life represents the fourth major cause of marriage failure. When couples enter marriage with a naïve perception of trials, it's not long before each partner begins to say, "Well, I must have married the wrong person. I never thought marriage would be like *this*." Doubt, division, and distance replace the unity and strength God desires for trials to produce in the marriage.

When this became an issue early in our marriage, we began a study of what God's Word had to say about trials, primarily because of our own desperate need. Our first reality shock came from reviewing 1 Peter 2:21: "For you have been called for this purpose, since Christ also suffered for you, leaving you an example for you to follow in His steps." The passage clearly teaches that God will allow Christians to suffer trials. God also gave us Christ as our model to overcome trials.

As Christians, we gladly accept the blessing of salvation through Christ's suffering. Yet we quickly reject any thought of joining in His suffering. Like the culture around us, we come to see our mission in life as avoiding pain or anything uncomfortable. But if our Lord suffered through trials, shouldn't we expect to experience them? The Bible teaches that God uses trials to cultivate the character of Christ in us. James explained that trials produce endurance, which leads to maturity. Therefore we are to "consider it all joy . . . when [we] encounter various trials" (James 1:2). The *joy* in this passage means a deep abiding peace that transcends difficult circumstances.

Sally and I repeatedly see couples in counseling who think their marriage is in trouble because of the trials they face. When they can't eliminate the trials, they attribute the resulting frustration and stress to their mate or marriage. *Blaming replaces unity.*

The truth is, life will almost always present us with trials. Most couples will experience them. Because they are so predictable, mental preparation is a must for wise couples. And though we can never be fully prepared for the unexpected, knowing that God is in control and that He has a plan for us can radically change the outcome. Recognizing suffering will come and giving thanks in the midst of it is a prerequisite to success in marriage.

When we got married, Sally had been a Christian for a number of years and was a very effective counselor on several college campuses. After a few years, our first child graced our home, followed by our second a year later. Through her contacts with students, Sally enjoyed a handy network of baby-sitters. The college girls needed the money, and Sally was able to continue her counseling ministries. It was a dream setup.

Shortly after our second child arrived, however, we moved to another city. With both children in diapers and each demanding more time and care, Sally's life totally changed. Her network of child-care help evaporated since it was difficult to become acquainted with people in the new neighborhood. My work required me to travel frequently, supervising staff in a large five-city area. The brunt of the move fell on Sally, who lost her counseling ministry, all her child-care support, and began a new era as a full-time mother.

My attitude was destroying what little self-respect she

had left.... Sally did pull through this difficult life change,

but with precious little help from me!

Her stress level skyrocketed. Often when I came home, her frustration was so high that we quickly had blowups, and I didn't understand why. Unresolved tension rapidly drained our "feelings" during this period. Like so many couples, we blamed the pain of life on each other, and we generalized: *All of the frustration is because of our marriage,* we thought.

I began to feel like Sally didn't love me. She sure wasn't much fun to be around anymore. I resented her negative changes when everything was going so well for me professionally—finding great success in my work, growing in the Christian life, and gaining respect among my peers. And since I didn't understand normal trials in life, it was as though I was blind to her sufferings. To make matters worse, I actually developed spiritual pride and said things like, "Sally, you've been acting like this for months! When are you going to snap out of it? What's the matter with you? You used to be such a stable Christian."

Actually, Sally was then—and is now—a godly woman, but my attitude was destroying what little self-respect she had left. The confidence she had in her relationship with Christ began to fade away. After much prayer and perseverance, Sally did pull through this difficult life change, but with precious little help from me! Having God's perspective on trials would have made things so much easier. We weren't out of God's will because we moved to another city, because we had two children so close together, or by our daily routines being changed so much. Instead, I failed to lift Sally up in the midst of this trial because we were unprepared for it.

Major lifestyle changes, such as having a child, moving, changing jobs, or even the death of a family member will trigger various degrees of trials. Daily living presents its own set of trials and sufferings. Isn't that what we confessed in our marriage vows when we said "for better or for worse, in sickness and in health?" So the issue is not how to avoid trials, but rather how to face them together.

Are you prepared to stand together? Having studied marriages for years, we have observed that trials stimulate growth in successful marriages. In less successful marriages, trials become a source of struggle, bitterness, and division. (In the final chapter, we will consider in depth how to confront some of the major trials in marriage.)

REASON FIVE:
Fantasy View of Love

With a troubled tone, Harry stammered, "After sixteen years of marriage, how could she fall in love with another man? How could she spend time alone with Jim? She should have known better. Now she wants him instead of me. I've been faithful; why can't she be?"

"It's his fault," Sue replied. "For two years he said he didn't care. I thought I would go crazy. Finally, in desperation, I turned to Jim and he was so understanding. We didn't plan on it, but we fell in love."

The fifth major cause of marriage failure today is what I call "fantasy love." It is based on feelings more than anything else. It is the kind of love we read about or see in movies and on television, represented by an emotional "high" that causes us to daydream and fantasize, or sends chills up our spines.

Most couples define love in terms of how they feel
There can be no weaker foundation for a relationship.

It is true that God created us with emotions, and they are an important element of human love. But *emotions are a terrible basis for a relationship.* The tragedy of fantasy love is that it is primarily based on feelings. If a person doesn't feel it anymore, he or she concludes that love has disappeared. Poof—it's gone! Like the couple I just mentioned, most couples today define love in terms of how they feel. There can be no weaker foundation for a relationship.

One of the primary contributors to fantasy love is unrestrained sexual expression. Our culture has encouraged the abuse of one of God's greatest gifts by encouraging people to prematurely become sexually active. Few issues can obscure an important decision more than sex. Encouraged by physical intimacy, emotions will flare instantly beyond normal proportions. Couples easily mistake lust for love. A relationship based solely on sex is bound for disaster. Today in a majority of troubled marriages, couples list sexual problems as one contributing factor. One study found that "virgin brides . . . are less likely to divorce than women who lost their virginity prior to marriage."[2] For many, these problems started long before their marriage began. Living together before marriage does not insure the adjustment or the relationship. Statistics prove just the opposite. "Couples who live together before marriage are about 48% more likely to divorce than those who don't," according to a *USA Today* article that reported the findings of a Rutgers University study. The research also found that unmarried couples have lower levels of happiness and a higher risk of domestic violence for the women.[3]

Some time ago a single woman came to ask my advice about a man with whom she was "terribly in love." I talked with her for about thirty minutes, and it was apparent she believed the relationship was really serious. At one point I made several suggestions on how to improve communications with her friend. Much to my surprise, she answered, "Oh, I haven't actually talked to him yet." Can you believe it? She had created a complete love relationship with a man she had never talked to! She was deeply in love with a myth! Today, easy access to the Internet allows long-distance computer love affairs with those we do not really know—the ultimate example of fantasy love!

Instead of risking the disappointment of rejection by a real person, some people create fantasies to bring them emotional pleasure. Not long ago I read in the newspaper that television soap operas have become such an important part of American women's lives that when news stories preempt the soap operas, the TV networks are deluged with complaints. The article went on to say that women are so caught up in these stories that when a marriage or death occurs on the screen, TV stations across the nation actually receive flowers or condolence cards. The end result of such fantasies is often personal mysticism and deep depression.

David's relationship with Bathsheba in the Old Testament is another example of fantasy love. As you recall, David had decided to stay home rather than fulfill his military duty. One day, while strolling on the palace roof, he noticed a woman bathing. He began to lust and have a fantasy relationship; then he had to have her. After learning who Bathsheba was, David had her husband, Uriah (a part of David's inner guard; 2 Samuel 23:8, 39), dispatched to war with sinister plans for him to purposely be killed. The ensuing affair would transform David into a liar, adulterer, and even a murderer. It is not an overstatement to say that affairs are based on lies and deception and may even lead to murder. They plunge honorable people into disgrace.

All fantasy love relationships, whether real or imagined, are simply counterfeit ways of trying to meet our needs. On the other hand, God's definition of love provides the real basis for permanent feelings. The Bible teaches that permanent feelings are only possible when couples learn to love by faith. Part 2 of this book describes that kind of love.

REASON SIX:
Lack of a Vital Relationship with Jesus Christ

According to Colossians 1:16, "All things have been created through Him and for Him." That includes marriage. Your marriage exists primarily to bring honor and glory to God. Even before you list your hopes, dreams, and needs for marriage, God is the first reason for your union. That's what it means to call Jesus Christ *preeminent:* He gets first place in all things, including your relationship.

The fundamental reason that a one partner marriage fails is a lack of a vital relationship with Jesus Christ in one marriage partner or both. Only Jesus Christ can unlock the deepest dimensions of human intimacy that occur at the spiritual level. If Jesus Christ does not dwell in your life, you're living at a reduced level of intimacy in your marriage. This is necessarily so since you're spiritually dead until Christ gives you life (see Ephesians 2:1). As shown in figure 2 (page 38), "Finding True Spiritual Intimacy," only Jesus Christ can take individuals and couples to their deepest level of intimacy—the intimacy of spirit.

Spiritual death in our lives limits intimacy in our marriages. Early in Genesis we see this principle at work. The death that God warned Adam about in Genesis 2:17 was realized later when the first couple together rebelled against God. Their fall in Genesis 3 did not bring immediate physical death. However, their fellowship was severed and they experienced spiritual death. Note that both Adam and Eve hid "themselves"; literally, their core selves were masked from God and one another. No longer did they enjoy the transparency and vulnerability described in Genesis 2:25. Instead, shame and blame replaced the perfect fellowship they once experienced.

You may experience various degrees of intimacy with one another physically, mentally, and emotionally in marriage. But only Jesus

Figure 2
Finding True Spiritual Intimacy

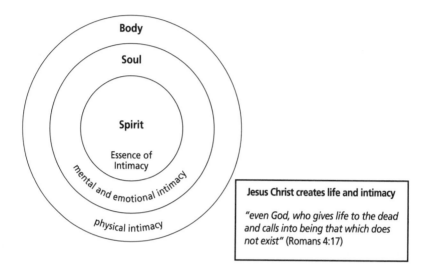

Christ can bring life to your core inner being—*your spirit*. Life at the spiritual level is most essential since God opens to the believing Christian a vast reservoir of supernatural capabilities for love, forgiveness, mercy, and all the fruits of the Holy Spirit. If you think you love your spouse now, just try loving him or her with the agape love of God!

The prerequisite to loving your spouse with God's agape love is maintaining a vibrant, intimate relationship with Jesus Christ. Many people know *about* God, have joined the church, been baptized, but really overlook knowing God *personally*. Others have become Christians and have a personal relationship with God through Christ, yet lack a vibrant, daily relationship with Him. Like getting to know a new friend, knowing God involves communicating with Him frequently, as well as having a growing appreciation for His attributes— holiness, mercy, love, kindness, and so on. When we know God in this intimate way, He is able to transform our lives by His love, thus equipping us to love our spouses even better.

It is possible to have Jesus Christ in your heart, but neglect a personal relationship with Him. To illustrate, suppose two people married, but immediately parted company after the wedding ceremony. One moved to New York and the other to Los Angeles, and the two lived with this arrangement for years. Are they legally married? Yes! But do they know one another very well? Hardly. Intimacy requires the investment of time and effort. It involves sharing yourself and becoming intimately acquainted with your spouse. Making Christ preeminent in your marriage requires that you first cultivate your intimate relationship with Him in your prayer life and Bible study time.

FROM GOOD INTENTIONS
TO CRITICISM AND FAILURE

As we noted earlier, good intentions cannot assure a successful marriage. Good intentions quickly give way to self-centered natures. As feelings subside, the couple slips into a fifty-fifty plan of responsibilities. Unsure that your mate is doing his part, you begin to watch your spouse's performance. A short list of observed failures begins to grow. You may soon conclude that you're stuck with a loser, an attitude certain to offend the mate. Critical attitudes deepen, and the cycle spins deeper and deeper. When you factor in trials common to most marriages, frustrations explode. Instead of standing together in adversity, the trials drive you farther apart as a couple.

So you see how easy it is for couples to plummet from marital bliss to shocking criticism and failure. Fantasy love has long evaporated, and they begin to think, "There's someone else out there who can better meet my needs."

The good news is that if you find yourself in this cycle, God has made a way for you to break free. If you're newly married, you don't have to get caught up in this destructive cycle. Regardless of how tempting each of the six reasons for marital failure noted above is, you can overcome all of them in Christ. Parts 2 and 3 will demonstrate that God not only created marriage; *He can make marriage work!*

NOTES

1. Larry Whitham, "Study of Successes Leads to Scoring of Couples' Chances," *The Washington Times,* 2 April 1996, A3.

2. "The Trouble with Premarital Sex," *U.S. News & World Report,* 19 May 1997, 60.

3. Karen S. Peterson, "Live-in Couples May Miss Out," *USA Today,* 1 February 1999, D1.

THREE

How the
Flame Fades

We often face couples whose dreams are being destroyed by one or more of the six factors discussed in chapter 2. Yet a person may understand all of the pitfalls and work to address them and still become ensnared in a problem marriage.

The flame that warmed romantic love and spurred a deeper love doesn't fade overnight; the fires and the dreams die *gradually and subtly*. In almost thirty years of working closely with couples and individuals, we have observed a progression toward bitterness and isolation in marriage that typically includes the following four stages:

- Stage One: The Days of Romance

- Stage Two: The Days of Reality

- Stage Three: The Days of Resentment

- Stage Four: The Days of Rebellion

While the stages are not absolute, they exist in most problem marriages. We could subtitle this chapter, "Predictable Stages of Marital Decline," as the stages are common and often cause the flame of marital love to flicker and fade. We will look at each.

STAGE ONE:
The Days of Romance

Our media is presently bombarding Americans with an unprecedented blitz that delivers one prevailing message: Experience the finest, most tantalizing things in life without taking personal responsibility. That is the ultimate fantasy, and its message comes constantly, delivered by the ever-present TV, and for the typical American, "six hundred advertising messages each day."[1] Years of this programming have resulted in a society that is looking for an *experience* or *romance*. The purpose of each message is to make you dissatisfied with what you have so you'll buy what the advertisers are selling.

Nowhere is this message clearer than the realm of romance. Marriage is portrayed as negative. Fantasy sex is portrayed as quick and positive. And love is confused with sex. Sex and love are greatly distorted from God's original purpose.

The values of our culture are diametrically opposed to God's values. These messages completely contradict the biblical teaching that love requires commitment. Only the Bible can offer a clear picture of marriage and family. The influence of Hollywood's values on our culture has been devastating. People are bound together on the basis of humanistic experiences or a rootless romanticism based on feelings. The result is that most marriages begin with each mate loaded with expectations that few spouses could ever fulfill.

During stage one, partners regard a good marriage as romance and often good sex as good marriage. The stage of romance typifies the first year of marriage, although this stage may last the first three years. Everything is bright and rosy; neither spouse is overly tired. (After all, there are no children, at least for the first nine months.) Romantic feelings prevail, and the pressures of job and home don't dominate.

This cultural worldview has set them up for disappointment and hurt. Since so many relationships are not grounded in the Word of God, the crash is swift and painful.

STAGE TWO:
The Days of Reality

The second stage usually occurs within the first three to five years of marriage, but may begin in the very first year. Sometimes the myths about sex and romance are destroyed before the honeymoon is over. Sooner or later, reality sets in. If there has been sex before marriage with one or more partners, sex within marriage just doesn't measure up.

Often reality is a harsh reminder of simply running out of time, as seen in the lives of Julie and Jim. Julie gets up by six, gets dressed, cooks, and is quickly off to work. After a hectic day at the office, she arrives home by six, fixes supper, eats, and finishes the dishes by eight. Washing clothes or house details may keep her busy until ten o'clock. By that time Julie is already thinking about getting up early the next morning, and she has had no real time for herself. Her husband Jim, oblivious to her workload, has been watching television all evening. By 10 P.M., he has fully relaxed after his busy workday; now he's ready for romance.

And Julie? Emotionally, Julie is unable to respond. Jim wonders what's wrong with her!

The euphoria of romance is quickly

replaced by the harsh realities of life....

Romance gives way to mediocrity.

Perhaps she is waiting for the day she can have children so she can stay at home. But when that day comes she will discover even greater pressure and responsibility. After several years, instead of experiencing marriage as a sexy honeymoon, Julie finds herself fighting for enough strength and personal time just to hold herself together.

Jim was idealistic when they married, a true believer in the romanticism of marriage. Deep in fantasy love, Jim loved to hold his sweetheart, and he thought his job was great. Before long, however, he became frustrated and unsure about his future. Changing jobs was not an option since he would likely have to return to a starting salary. Now he feels pressure from Julie, who doesn't want to feel trapped by financial circumstances, and he doesn't want to upset her even more.

So the euphoria of romance is quickly replaced by the harsh realities of life. Fantasy love gives way to job pressures and money problems. As children come along, they demand an even greater commitment. Romance gives way to mediocrity.

During this sobering stage, feelings begin to wane. Depression overtakes joy and contentment. Romantic zeal fades. This can be catastrophic since the fantasy feelings were the primary basis for the marriage. Frequent expressions of love disappear, followed by an unwillingness to serve the other. Left unchecked, a scary feeling settles into the pit of Jim and Julie's stomachs that they may have made a mistake by marrying each other.

STAGE THREE:
The Days of Resentment

When feelings have changed and creative, sacrificial acts disappear, marriage partners begin to deeply resent each other. Blaming begins with statements like "You *never* talk to me anymore," or "We *never* have sex anymore," or "You *always* . . ." It becomes obvious when one partner has reached the point of feeling "stuck" with his or her mate. The one who feels stuck resents the other's inadequacies and may even resent God for allowing the marriage to occur. The other mate feels judged, rejected, and misunderstood, which quickly degenerates into anger. Thus the cycle of resentment has begun.

When couples reach this point of deep resentment, they begin to lose hope. If they don't get help, they typically move in one of two directions. First, they may tragically move toward *divorce*. Since there is so little stigma in divorce today, many couples just give up and get out! But divorce is rarely the answer. All too often it only leads to more frustration, depression, and financial hardship. And then these couples usually remarry, only to carry with them emotional baggage and the extremely difficult adjustments of blending families.

The second direction is the *compromised marriage*. A large segment of marriages today fit into this category. A compromised marriage is one in which people don't really deal with their mistakes, attitudes, weaknesses, and differences. Instead, each goes his or her own way and purposely avoids the volatile areas of the marriage. It's a pretend marriage. On the surface, they appear to be all right, but inside they harbor deep resentment. Occasionally the pressure may build until the couple explode in anger. Several days of frustration will end with a statement similar to this: "Well, I wish things were different. But I am not going to end the relationship because of what it would do to the children. So, I'll just put up with the problems." Try as they will, compromised couples cannot prosper over the long haul.

Sexual dysfunction often appears in a compromised marriage. The wife may be so disillusioned that she simply has no sexual appetite. For instance, Matt is aware that his wife, Brenda, is aloof, even cold to him. He tries to ignore her passivity at first, but on a particular night, he observes Brenda undressing and his attraction cannot be restrained. Tired and resentful of Matt's lack of attention earlier in the evening, she refuses his advances. Matt explodes. Brenda feels angry and guilty at the same time. They fall asleep on opposite sides of the bed and awaken the next morning to "no comment."

Many supposedly successful marriages are really

just two people going their own independent ways,

being careful not to step on each other's toes.

Or consider the wife who is raising the children with a husband who is never home or remains uninvolved. Sharon sees personality or discipline problems developing in her children daily, and she cannot bear the burdens alone. Since she knows her husband resents her for saying anything, she tries to ignore the problems. One night John, who hasn't spent meaningful time with the children in weeks, gets angry with them, yells, and even spanks them. Unable to stand it, Sharon explodes, and the gap in the marriage widens.

Sadly, many supposedly successful marriages are really just two people going their own independent ways, being careful not to step on each other's toes. The husband loses himself in his work to compensate for the lack of respect at home. The wife becomes consumed with the children to compensate for the lack of intimacy within the marriage.

Compromised marriages often rock along until the partners reach their late forties or early fifties, and the children leave home. The true measure of their relationship comes when all they have is each other. Ultimately, most compromised relationships lead to deeper and deeper resentment. If not checked, resentment will destroy a person's life like a cancer.

STAGE FOUR:
The Days of Rebellion

Unresolved resentment impacts men and women differently. Women typically become critical, and then fearful. Men become hardened and uncaring. For a season, resentment may simmer behind the illusion of a healthy marriage, fueled by unmet needs. Sooner or later, however, the compounding resentment explodes into overt acts of rebellion against the spouse.

The soured marriage was constantly on her mind. . . .

Paula greeted each day with a fear of failure and an

increasingly critical attitude toward Steve.

Paula entered marriage with deep romantic feelings for Steve. She viewed him with trust, placing him high on a pedestal. She dreamed of a model home and children. Her body was young and her self-image was at a peak.

But after several years of marriage, her dreams had turned to nightmares. She and Steve had failed to cope with reality in their marriage, and resentment consumed each of them. Her feelings for

Steve were distant history. She not only didn't trust Steve, but she criticized his every move. Along with bearing children, the stress of the marriage had taken a toll on her once attractive figure. She didn't even like herself anymore. Her days often seemed burdensome, long, and introspective. The soured marriage was constantly on her mind. Rather than facing the future with confidence, Paula greeted each day with a fear of failure and an increasingly critical attitude toward Steve.

What a sad picture. With two children, ages seven and four, Paula knows the tremendous personal responsibility they will demand over the next fifteen years. By then she will be forty-five and her youthful years will be long gone. All that will be left is a husband for whom she has lost her enthusiasm.

Paula has subconsciously become *fearful* and *depressed*. Fearful, hurting people sometimes take desperate actions to regain a sense of control in their lives. Often that action comes in the form of rebellion against God and the mate. Often in counseling wives say something like, "Life is no fun anymore," or "I don't enjoy people like I used to," or "So-and-so (another man) makes me feel so alive and appreciated." God created women and men in such a way that they require hope. Without it, rebellion can erupt into all kinds of behavior that will deliver the final blow to the marriage.

Steve, like most men, responded to his unresolved resentment differently. He hardened his feelings toward others, including his mate. He had become more *insensitive* and *self-centered* in their relationship. How different from when they first married. During the first months, Steve would have literally died for Paula. But as she became more aware of Steve's weaknesses, Paula increasingly criticized his actions. Steve's sense of self-confidence as the spiritual leader in his home plummeted. Feelings of failure replaced courage and creativity. Faced with Paula's growing criticism, Steve retreated. His respect for her was soon replaced with disgust and avoidance. How far can the stage of rebellion lead a man in his calloused disregard for his wife? Some years ago Carl showed me just how far.

After Carl entered my office for counseling, I quickly learned he and Alice had been married twenty years. As I listened, I was impressed with how romantic the early years of marriage were for this couple. With the passing of time, however, Alice's domineering personality made her critical of his every move. She frequently humiliated him by correcting him in public. Increasingly she sowed seeds of disrespect. At the time Carl came to my office, the two had separated.

As Carl's story unfolded, I could tell he had layers of resentment and bitterness deep inside. Over the next few weeks, Alice and Carl alternated with counseling appointments, but they never came together.

Not long after our first few appointments, Alice called me from the hospital to say that she was having emergency cancer surgery. She was terribly frightened, and asked if I would call Carl and ask him to visit her.

When I finally reached Carl, he was preparing to leave town on a deep-sea fishing trip. After I explained Alice's medical emergency, he replied, "That woman has been controlling my life for twenty years. I don't care if she dies and goes to hell; she isn't going to ruin my fishing trip!" And he hung up. Here was a man who worshiped his wife early in marriage, but now had become hardened against her. For Carl, rebellion took the shape of breaking her heart and spirit at a time when she most needed him.

But remember: Carl's heart didn't become calloused overnight. If not corrected, the patterns of fearfulness for women and hardness for men will deteriorate until both mates begin to think that the *best of life was missed because of their spouse.* The cancer of bitterness is predictable, progressive, and will become overwhelming. Don't play around with unresolved bitterness and resentment. You may think you have it under control today; tomorrow it may blow up in your face. *The spark of love and commitment fades one incident at a time.* Has bitterness taken root in your heart and marriage?

THE ULTIMATE SOLUTION

How can we as couples avoid moving to stages three and four? Sadly, even Christians can move into these later stages when God is not the center of their lives. But it need not be that way. Although all couples will experience the first two stages of romanticism and reality, stages three and four—resentment and rebellion—are not automatic. In fact, as the disillusionment of the reality stage sets in, every couple will arrive at a critical crossroads in their relationship: turn to God in faith, or begin the slippery slide into resentment and rebellion.

Submitting to Christ's love will allow you to have dominion over your self-centeredness and sin. As Christians, your mate and you can now find oneness in marriage and a new beginning by drawing closer to Christ.

What if you are not a Christian? Then the ultimate solution to stages three and four is to come to Christ in faith. Breaking the cycle of bitterness and resentment rooted deep within the human heart has only one cure: literally being saved by the Lord Jesus Christ. When you turn to Christ in faith, you literally access divine resources to keep your love fresh for one another.

A man once asked, "Don, is it necessary to mention God when discussing my marriage problems?" We had just spent several hours discussing the four stages of a declining marriage. I answered his question with a question of my own.

"Mike, as we have talked about you and Judy, your struggles, conflicts, and rejection of each other, you said you could not seem to control your actions. Why?"

"I don't know," Mike replied.

"Two people who are egocentric and self-centered will naturally struggle," I explained. "When their feelings fade, they have no natural basis upon which to build a relationship. Frankly, only Jesus Christ can provide a lasting basis for your relationship, Mike."

----------------- ⌒⌒ -----------------

Receiving the life and power

of the Lord Jesus Christ . . . is the only true hope

for restoring a marriage.

----------------- ⌒⌒ -----------------

"Yes, but I've heard all that before. Being a Christian didn't stop our friends Bill and Joyce from getting a divorce."

"Mike," I replied, "don't reject Christ's love and power because of some hypocrisy or downfall you've seen in someone else. God continues to love us even when we reject Him. Christ died for your sins so you could have eternal life. If you and Judy establish a relationship with Him, He will provide you both a foundation for your marriage, as well as the power to break out of these negative behaviors. Lasting relationships occur best when couples become 'one' in Christ. If you turn to Christ in humility, He will make you a child of God."

So it is for everyone. Receiving the life and power of the Lord Jesus Christ—the Bible calls it being "born again"—is the only true hope for restoring a marriage. Here's what the Bible tells you to do in order to accept Christ as Lord and Savior in your life.

1. Acknowledge that God has a wonderful plan for your life. God Himself has said that. "'For I know the plans that I have for you,' declares the Lord, 'plans for welfare and not for calamity to give you a future and a hope'" (Jeremiah 29:11).

2. Confess to God that you have missed His plan by living without Him. The Bible calls this sin. "For all have sinned and fall short of the glory of God" (Romans 3:23).

3. Accept the biblical truth that as the eternal Son of God, Jesus Christ died on a cross for your sins, was buried, and resurrected from the dead. "For I delivered to you as of first importance what I also received, that Christ died for our sins according to the Scriptures, and that He was buried, and that He was raised on the third day according to the Scriptures" (1 Corinthians 15:3–4).

4. On the basis of Christ's work on the cross, ask God to forgive you of all your sins. "If we confess our sins, He is faithful and righteous to forgive us our sins and to cleanse us from all unrighteousness" (1 John 1:9). This means you want Him to save you from your selfishness.

5. By faith, receive Jesus Christ into your life. "But as many as received Him, to them He gave the right to become children of God, even to those who believe in His name" (John 1:12).

"That if you confess with your mouth Jesus as Lord, and believe in your heart that God raised Him from the dead, you will be saved" (Romans 10:9).

If you have never taken the step of committing your life to Christ, we encourage you to do so right now. In the quietness of your heart, pray something like, "Lord Jesus, I need You. Please come into my heart and life right now and forgive my sin. Thank You for dying on the cross for me. Teach me how to live the Christian life. Help me to become a godly husband/wife. Thank You for coming into my life. In Jesus' name, amen."

If you believe these biblical truths and have sincerely prayed the prayer above, you are now a child of God. Jesus has come to live in your life for all time and eternity. God says, "And the testimony is this, that God has given us eternal life, and this life is in His Son. He who has the Son has the life; he who does not have the Son of God does not have the life" (1 John 5:11–12).

Submitting to Christ's love will allow you to have dominion over your self-centeredness and sin. You and your mate can now find oneness in marriage and a new beginning in life through Christ.

The balance of this book is designed to train you how to draw close to God in faith, apply principles from His Word to your marriage, and avoid the descent into resentment and rebellion.

FROM RESENTMENT AND REBELLION ...TO DISSOLUTION

No spouse wants to move to stages three and four, resentment and rebellion. Yet after the stage of reality sets in, many couples (either one or both partners) respond with resentment, moving to stage three. They want their partner to give his or her 50 percent of responsibilities. This quickly turns into a critical inspection of the spouse; and a short list of observed failures begins to grow.

Soon each partner feels stuck with the other, which simply heightens the hurt and rejection. Once all alternatives have been exhausted, the couple admits there is a problem.

In addition to the sometimes painful realities that dash our romantic expectations, couples typically have to deal with a constant barrage of trials. Instead of standing unified, trials become just another occasion to assign blame for more failures in our mates. Couples soon arrive at a point where they can't remember why they married in the first place.

In just a few short years, a couple can slide from marital bliss to the shocking reality of rejection. Without a godly solution, long-term struggles settle into a compromised marriage where both partners agree to disagree. But since compromise doesn't solve the problems, resentment and bitterness grow into rebellion. The dissolution of the marriage is just around the corner.

To *desire* to love is natural. To *really* love is supernatural. If God designed marriage, can He make it work? Parts 2 and 3 will demonstrate that *God can and does make marriage work.*

NOTE

1. Richard A. Swenson, *Margin: Restoring Emotional, Physical, Financial, and Time Reserves to Overloaded Lives* (Colorado Springs: Navpress, 1995) 85, 150.

PART TWO

How to Make Lasting Commitments in Marriage

FOUR

God's Plan, Man's Hope

Suppose you become sick at work one day with a variety of symptoms: nausea, fever, aches and pains, red rashes, and profuse sweating. Alarmed, you go straight to the doctor, where he performs a variety of tests. After a thorough examination, the doctor makes the diagnosis and prescribes several prescription drugs. But once at home, you line up the prescription bottles on the kitchen counter and leave them there without taking the first pill.

What good did it do to visit the doctor if you don't follow his directions to regain your health? What good is it to submit to medical tests? Why bother to have prescriptions filled if you won't take the medication? None of these steps can help you regain your health unless you're willing to do what the doctor says.

Reading books about marriage won't automatically change your marriage. Neither will attending seminars or completing workbooks. If you want your marriage to improve, you must *apply* the principles you learn from God's Word. After more than three decades of marriage counseling, one thing has become very clear to us: *There* is usually very little difference between Christian marriages and non-Christian marriages. Christians may start out with the best of intentions for themselves and their mates. But unless they are willing to *apply*—that is, commit to obeying—the principles they hear, not much will change.

A successful marriage is not guaranteed by a good beginning; it can occur only when *two people daily apply God's Word to their marriage*. Marital oneness requires two people who each possess a supernatural mind-set, a perspective granted from God. As these two people obey the Lord and His Word, their faith will be rewarded with the blessing of oneness.

Marital oneness requires first *knowing* something, then *acting* on what one knows, followed by *persevering* through faith. In part 2 we will learn what God wants us to *know* about how and why He created marriage. In part 3 we will learn how to *apply* what we know to various practical areas of marriage.

SIN AND HUMAN RELATIONSHIPS

Before we discuss three reasons why God created mankind and marriage, it is essential to properly set the biblical context. The early chapters of Genesis describe the original marriage and how sin marred Adam and Eve's relationship with God, thus affecting all humans. Studying Genesis 1–3, we can make several fundamental observations before we can fully appreciate God's plan for marriage.

- Genesis 1–2 describe a time when sin and self-centeredness did not exist. Both Adam and Eve were perfect and pure when God spoke these words. As we read those two chapters, we conclude that God's perfect intent for mankind and marriage are clearly stated.

- Genesis 3 introduces mankind's rebellion against God. Because of sin, every relationship became distorted: relationships between God and mankind, all human relationships, mankind and nature, and even a person's relationship to himself. According to Isaiah 14:12–17 and Ezekiel 28:2–5; 12–19, God's authority was challenged by a fallen angel named Lucifer (Satan), who planned to make himself like God. In the verses above, Lucifer declared that he didn't need God to experience life. He set himself up as God and became independent from God. This reality is important because part of God's purpose in creating mankind and the resulting marriages was to demonstrate that only *dependence on God* can bring fulfillment and success in life. Satan is still in the business of enticing people into independence *from* God.

• Marriage was the first social institution God created, preceding even His relationship with Israel and the church. In marriage, Adam and Eve were blessed with a responsibility to carry out God's great purposes (described in the next section). If you are married, then you are also blessed with those same awesome responsibilities before God. Thus, your marriage is not an accident or afterthought of God. Instead, it is the basic foundation of all social structure on earth. Adam and Eve, and every couple that has followed, have a tremendous stake in God's plan of the ages.

• To fulfill these God-given purposes, it is essential that every couple become completely dependent on God Himself. Adam and Eve's dependence on God, as opposed to Satan's independence, was vital! Yet through the ages, Satan still uses the same tactics: His desire is to lead rebellion and independence against God. Our purpose is to help you stand firm against this lie. As we consider God's plan, we must recognize the important part our marriages play in that plan. Let's see what our responsibility is.

GOD'S THREE PURPOSES
FOR MEN AND WOMEN

With this background, let's look specifically at why God created men and women and the institution of marriage. Genesis 1 describes all of creation. Verses 1–25 describe the creation of the heavens, the earth, vegetation, and animals; our focus will be on verses 26–31, which describe the creation of mankind. Here God's Word indicates three great purposes for men and women, to: (1) reflect God's image, (2) reproduce after their kind, and (3) reign over the creation.

The first reason God created marriage was for men and women to reflect His image together as a couple. That becomes clear in reading verses 26–27: "Then God said, 'Let Us make man in *Our image, according to Our likeness;* and let them rule over the fish of the sea and over the birds of the sky and over the cattle and over all the earth, and over every creeping thing that creeps on the earth.' God created man in His own *image,* in the *image of God* He created him; male and female He created them" (italics added).

Three times God uses the word "image" and once "likeness" to stress that *He wants mankind to reflect His image.* From the plural pronouns "Us" and "Our" used in verse 26, it is clear that God intended mankind to reflect the wholeness of the Trinity: the Father, Son, and Holy Spirit. Each person of the Trinity is unique in function, yet one in nature and purpose. The concept of reflecting God's light to a lost world is common in Scripture and can be found in passages such as Matthew 5:13–16 and Isaiah 60:1–5. What a privilege that God would choose to reveal Himself to the world through your marriage relationship!

Verse 27 contains a very important delineation about mankind: God mentions that "male and female He created them." Even though God made Adam and Eve to individually reflect His image, it is also true that together, in a profound and mysterious way, they would be able to reflect the *unity* or the *oneness* of God (see John 17:20–21 and Ephesians 5:31–32).

(So what about singles? Singles can reflect the image of God as they join in oneness with the church or the body of Christ. However, since this book is about marriage, we won't explore God's plan for singles, even though they too are called to reflect God's image in His church, made up of men and women.)

In marriage, couples best reflect God's image by *becoming one.* By creating Adam and Eve as the parents of humanity, God desired for them to model oneness to all who would follow. When couples reflect oneness, God is truly glorified. On the other hand, when strife replaces unity in marriage, the couple miss their greatest opportunity to reflect a loving God. Nothing in life is more tragic than being married and failing to reflect the unity of God's image. Incredibly, most couples are not even aware of God's plan for them to reflect Him!

A second tragedy in our generation is society's distortion of maleness and femaleness. The distinction between the two genders is under severe attack as the drive for a politically correct "unisex" society increases. Men and women desire to be like one another. Dress and roles have become blurred between the two. Each gender is in an identity crisis, resulting in unthinkable confusion and suffering. This is not the kind of unity God desires. As a result, even the ability to reflect God's image has suffered. Did He make a mistake? Certainly not! Each gender is vital. God is honored when a man and a woman unite to reveal His likeness and unity. God's plan is for masculinity and femininity to be distinct.

Men and women, God is instructing you from the Genesis passage that oneness in your marriage is not optional. If you hope to please God, then you must reflect His image. His reflection requires a union between maleness and femaleness. If God has indeed called you out of singleness into marriage, you and your mate must understand and experience God's eternal purpose.

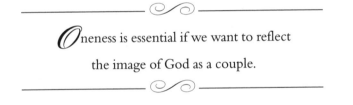

Oneness is essential if we want to reflect the image of God as a couple.

Today many people seem uncertain about these ideas, either trying to decide whether to marry or if married, whether to divorce. Most are not aware that God has a plan for their marriage. Because Sally and I are committed to reflecting God's image through our marriage, divorce is not an option. I would be incomplete without my wife. To lose her through divorce would limit my ability to fully reflect God's image, according to the Scripture. Since I have learned God's purpose of reflecting Him in marriage, Sally's importance to me has multiplied in innumerable ways. Oneness is essential if we want to reflect the image of God as a couple.

The second purpose for mankind and marriage is to reproduce after our kind. Genesis 1:28 records: "God blessed them [Adam and Eve]; and God said to them, 'Be fruitful and multiply, and fill the earth.'"

No question here. God designed marriage to produce children, whom God regards as a blessing second only to the marriage relationship itself. The word *blessing* refutes any notion that God created marital sexual expression in a negative light. He blessed Adam and Eve's sexual union as another way of reflecting His unity in marriage.

With more than six billion people on the earth, you may think this purpose for marriage has been met. But look again. God's plan was not only for marriages to reflect His image and produce children. He also desires for our children to reproduce after our kind; that is, *to reflect His image.*

This purpose could also be stated, "Reproduce a godly heritage that will also reflect God's image." First, God told Adam and Eve to reflect His image. Next, God told them to increase that reflection through godly offspring. Adam and Eve together were to produce one small light on this huge earth. By reproducing godly children (who love, honor, and obey God), God desired that Adam and Eve's reflection be increased—eventually exceeding six billion lights. They were intended to be people just like you and me, who would reflect the truth that only dependence on God brings real life.

In this way, God has made marriage a strategic element in seeing the fulfillment of the Great Commission spoken by Jesus in Matthew 28:19–20: "Go therefore and *make disciples* of all the nations, baptizing them in the name of the Father and the Son and the Holy Spirit, teaching them to observe all that I commanded you; and lo, I am with you always, even to the end of the age" (italics added). And marriage becomes a model as well: In the same way we nurture children at home, we are to nurture and train disciples of Jesus to further God's kingdom here on earth.

God's third purpose for mankind is stated in the second half of Genesis 1:28, to "subdue [the earth]; and rule over . . . every living thing." God intended for Adam and Eve to rule or have dominion over the earth and its creatures. God makes it clear throughout Scripture that He wants married couples to take charge of everything that He has given them dominion over, including property, each mate's spiritual gifts, their children, financial income and assets, as well as social and political influences. All earthly resources are to be used as God's Spirit directs in order to bring honor to God.

God's charge to "subdue and rule" the earth includes not only the physical domain but the spiritual realm as well. Throughout the Old and New Testaments, the Holy Spirit exhorts believers to "be strong and courageous" (e.g., Joshua 1:6, 7, 9), "put on the full armor of God," and to "stand firm against the schemes of the devil" (Ephesians 6:11). God is honored as we exhibit victories in the spiritual realm for the sake of Christ. *Oneness in marriage is essential if we want to reign on planet Earth and bring glory to God.*

APPLYING GOD'S PURPOSES

In summary, God's plan for your marriage requires each of you to be dependent upon Him. You are called to (1) reflect His image, (2) raise godly children, and (3) reign over the earth. Your faith in God demonstrates to all creation that the only way to experiencing a fulfilled life now, as well as eternal life in the future, is through complete dependence upon Him.

In marriage, you will not accomplish these three goals unless each of you has a personal relationship with Jesus Christ as Savior. Every day couples marry with the intention of finding fulfillment apart from God, and the results are evident. As we noted in chapter 3, the ultimate solution is Jesus Christ within; He meets our deepest needs for spiritual intimacy and purpose in our marriages. No one can reflect the image of God and fulfill His purposes for marriage without God's help.

For Christians, goal one, *reflecting God's image,* requires oneness with our spouse, and that, in turn, requires the ongoing work of Jesus Christ. Will non-Christians really be attracted to God through your example if you are divided as a couple? Absolutely not!

Similarly, *we can reproduce healthy, successful, and godly children* only by being one with our mates. When questioned, children consistently say that the most important aspect of family life is the way Mom and Dad love each other. When divided parents attempt to discipline children, without realizing it, they create opposite poles in their children. It's no wonder children take the opposite position from their parents at a later stage in life. Couples are shocked to learn that their lack of oneness in marriage has modeled division. Apart from oneness, child rearing is like grasping the wind.

Finally, we can attain *the third goal of reigning* over the physical earth when as a couple we are one. This is part of God's plan for couples: to effectively rule their unified resources for God's honor and to stand together in spiritual battle. Why should God increase your influence in the culture if you haven't faithfully managed what He has already given you? (See, for instance, Luke 16:10–11.)

You may have great plans, but they will be frustrated by division in your marriage. Can you handle the tremendous pressures of life without another to lean on? (Note Ecclesiastes 4:9–10). Maybe you can manage momentary pressure, but a lifetime of handling pressure alone will take a huge toll. Our outlook on life becomes warped under the incessant pressures of life. To adequately handle this battle, we need our spouses holding us up through prayer and spiritual encouragement.

When Sally and I married, we had not discovered God's purposes for marriage. Therefore the Holy Spirit could not call upon these Scriptures to convict us of our division, and we suffered terribly as a result. God's image, poorly reflected by us, suffered as well.

Since our discovering God's plans for marriage, the Holy Spirit can now instantly remind us when we falter in our oneness. Sally and I simply cannot reflect, reproduce, or reign without oneness in our marriage first. We literally shudder at the thought of not being one with each other.

What we fear most, though, is the thought of displeasing the heart of God—the same One who created us and sent Christ to die for us; the God who loves us to the end, in spite of how undeserving we are. If we are not one—unified—we are blocking His plan and missing the opportunity to reflect Him to others.

God is unchanging: "Jesus Christ is the same yesterday and today and forever" (Hebrews 13:8). Therefore, His plan for marriage is the same today as it was for Adam and Eve. We are either going to believe it, or we won't. We will either follow His plan and experience abundant life, or we won't. *Oneness in marriage is not an option.* It's essential.

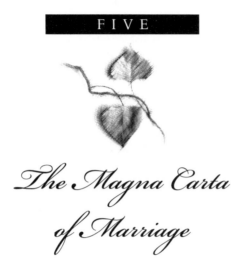

FIVE

The Magna Carta of Marriage

As we saw in Genesis 1:26–28, God viewed the first couple as one. He refers to the male and female as "them," ("let them rule" and "God blessed them"); the pronoun indicates that God regarded them as one, as illustrated by the Godhead described in the plural pronouns "Us" and "Our" of Genesis 1:26. In fact, their ability to reflect God, reproduce, and reign was dependent on their oneness. If oneness is a prerequisite to success in marriage, then how can we accomplish such unity?

The answer to that question is found in Genesis 2, where God reveals the creation of mankind with Adam and Eve. They were the world's first couple as well as history's first marriage. Through them, God intended to show every couple who would follow what it meant to *become one*. Apart from verses that teach salvation and the ministry of the Holy Spirit, Genesis 2 has had more impact on our life and marriage than any other single passage of Scripture. Don't miss what God has for you in this key chapter. Genesis 2 is the Magna Carta of Marriage; it is God's blueprint for marriage.

In Genesis 2 we read the directions for marriage written by the Creator of marriage. The point of Genesis 1 is that married people can best fulfill God's purposes for creation (reflect, reproduce, reign) by being one with their mate. Genesis 2 is crucial because it tells us *how* to experience it.

In Genesis 2:18, God reveals a principle that is critical for experiencing oneness in marriage: God insures unity in the marriage by creating each person with needs that He meets through the life of the mate. God has created me with needs that He meets through Sally. Sally has needs that God meets in her life through me. Importantly, only *as we each submit to God* can He direct us in meeting one another's needs.

Experiencing this principle in real life involves recognizing four specific steps in how God provides for our personal needs. Those four steps, found in Genesis 2 and depicted in figure 3, are discussed in the next section.

GOD CREATES A NEED

At the time of creation, Adam was different from you and me in several ways. First, he had no sin. Adam also lived in a *perfect physica environment*. Finally, and most importantly, Adam had a *perfect relationship* with the living God. Adam could actually experience God with

Figure 3
Four Steps in God's Meeting of Our Needs

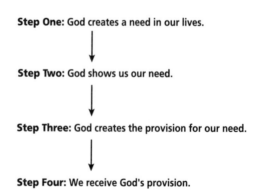

Step One: God creates a need in our lives.

Step Two: God shows us our need.

Step Three: God creates the provision for our need.

Step Four: We receive God's provision.

two of his five senses. He could *see* the Shekinah glory of God as Moses would later see, and he could actually *hear* God speak. Scripture says that Adam walked and talked with God. Everything seemed to be just right for Adam.

Yet in verse 18, for the first time in all creation, God observes that something was "not good." "Then the Lord God said, 'It is not good for the man to be alone; I will make him a helper suitable for him'" (Genesis 2:18). It was not good for Adam to be alone. Notice that Adam did not complain to God about being alone. The thought never occurred to him; *God indicated* that Adam was alone. In calling attention to Adam's aloneness, God emphasized very clearly that man was not yet complete. In other words, God was not finished with His creation.

He [God] chose to create a need in mankind for human relationships in addition to fellowship with God.

Adam was unable to reflect God's image by himself. Man was not created to stand alone, then or now. By God's wise design, He chose to create a need in mankind for human relationships in addition to fellowship with God. Thus, from the beginning of human history, *relationships are not an option*. The pattern, established by God, has not changed because of time or culture.

This need for human relationship in no way lessens our need for and dependence upon God. Everything that God creates is designed to increase our dependence upon Him. God could have created Eve simultaneously with Adam. But to insure dependence upon Himself, God clearly showed Adam his need *first* so he would trust God for the fulfillment of that need. Thus Adam began a life of total trust in the perfect plan of the Most High.

The word *suitable* means "to complete or to correspond to." This was God's way of saying that Adam was incomplete. In Genesis 1, God continually referred to human beings as "they" and "them." It is clear that God saw Adam and Eve as a *single unit of two*. Don't overlook this key insight!

After God observed that Adam was alone, you would expect to see God create Eve, right? *Wrong!* Instead, God assigned Adam a project that would clearly reveal the man's need for a helper: "Out of the ground the Lord God formed every beast of the field and every bird of the sky, and brought them to the man to see what he would call them; and whatever the man called a living creature, that was its name. The man gave names to all the cattle, and to the birds of the sky, and to every beast of the field, but for Adam there was not found a helper suitable for him" (Genesis 2:19–20).

GOD SHOWS US OUR NEED

What a shock! Instead of Eve, God brought all the animals to Adam. Why? The answer is found in the last part of verse 20: "but for Adam there was not found a helper suitable for him." God rarely gives us anything without first showing us our need. Remember that everything in creation is designed by God to increase our dependence upon Him.

Adam, however, initially didn't know what aloneness was. From his perspective, everything was perfect. As a result, he could not have fully appreciated Eve at this point. So how did Adam discover his need through naming animals?

To begin with, animals don't talk! He named the first and proceeded to the next. Same response. None of them spoke. Was he beginning to see a need? Animal after animal was named, yet not one could communicate with him. And surely he noticed that there were two of every animal, yet each was made differently. The animals were paired off—animal families, if you will. Most importantly, Adam learned there was no creature suitable for (similar to, corresponding to) him. There was no one to talk to, no one to eat with, and no one to complete him as a companion. The point is, *we must see our need before we can appreciate the provision for that need.*

I remember being so excited when my son, Todd, was born. I bought a football and took it to him while he was still in the hospital. Of course, he didn't appreciate it, since he had no need for a football as a newborn!

Well, I'm a slow learner. On Todd's fourth Christmas, I decided it was time for him to learn to ride a bicycle. I had always pictured

Todd on a bike. Christmas Day found Todd excited about the bike, but it only lasted about two hours. In the months that followed, the bike sat unused in the garage. *He didn't have a need for a bike.*

When Todd was six, we moved to Little Rock, and he soon observed a neighbor boy riding a very special bike—a sporty black bike, without training wheels and with mud tires. Todd excitedly ran in, exclaiming, "Daddy, I've got to have a bike like Brent's!" Even though I was a slow learner, I was beginning to catch on.

"Todd," I said, "Daddy would love for you to have a bike like Brent's, but if you remember, you haven't ridden the other bike very much, and bikes cost a lot of money."

So Todd rode his bike without training wheels for four months, praying daily to the Lord for a "big bike like Brent's." Not one night passed in four months that Todd didn't pray for that bike. We were amazed at the fact that Todd didn't want to go to bed without praying. Before this, we encouraged him to pray, but he could never think of anything to say.

As Christmas neared, we were short of money. Sally told Todd that he would need to pray for our finances, especially to make our house payment. So Todd prayed earnestly for the house payment *and the bike.* As parents, we learned a lot about prayer from the faith of a child.

About a week before Christmas, a large, unexpected check arrived. Todd was not at all surprised. He *expected* God to answer. On Christmas morning, Todd found his big black and yellow bike with mud tires under the tree! How real God was becoming to him. His thrill with the bike didn't wane in two months or even the next two years. Todd cleaned and polished that bike and put it in the garage every night. It was very special to him because it was *God's provision* for a need that he had.

Do you see your need for your mate? Maybe you realized that fact when you were single, but do you realize how your mate fills your needs now? And are you sure how your mate needs you? God showed Adam his need *before* giving Eve to him so that he could fully appreciate, care for, and cherish God's gift. Certainly a worthy goal for every couple during the engagement period is to clearly understand their need for one another. Interestingly, married couples report they see more and more their need for each other as the years progress.

GOD CREATES THE
PROVISION FOR OUR NEED

Now we're getting to the exciting part. Having first created Adam with a need for a relationship, and then having shown him his need, God now creates Eve to meet Adam's need. Genesis 2:21–22 records that "the Lord God caused a deep sleep to fall upon the man, and he slept; then He took one of his ribs and closed up the flesh at that place. The Lord God fashioned into a woman the rib which He had taken from the man, and brought her to the man."

God caused Adam to sleep while He created Eve. This is a beautiful picture of God's part—meeting our needs—and man's part—resting in God's promises. Most of us couples are not resting in God. Rather, we are actively looking, inspecting the assembly line of "Eves" and "Adams"—hoping to find the perfect one. Yet it is God who provides for our needs, both before and during marriage.

We've heard it said that God chose a rib to signify the perfect picture of the husband–wife relationship. The woman is under the protection of the man's arm but protects the man's most vital part— his heart. Eve was not taken from his head to rule over him, nor from his feet to be beneath him, but was formed alongside him to complete him, and vice versa. Husbands and wives are to be "fellow heir[s] of the grace of life" (1 Peter 3:7) as companions, lovers, friends, and parents.

The most strategic statement in the passage seems odd at first. God "*brought* her to [Adam]." It seems God would have created Eve right next to Adam. Why did He bring her to Adam? God wanted Adam to know that just as it was God who had created her, it was also God *alone* who would *present* her to him as the greatest gift. For the unmarried, we believe God asks today, "Will you trust Me to bring your mate to you?" For the married, He asks, "Will you thank Me for the mate I have given you?" God desires complete dependence on Him for all our needs, be that before or after marriage.

WE RECEIVE GOD'S PROVISION

Such a great gift—our spouse—we should receive gladly. Notice how Adam embraced God's provision: "This is now bone of my bones, and flesh of my flesh; she shall be called Woman, because she was taken out of Man" (Genesis 2:23). The English text does not fully communicate Adam's excitement. A better translation of the Hebrew would be, "Great! Fantastic! Thank You, Lord! I'll take her!" Adam was 100 percent excited about her. Adam *totally* received Eve.

Was it Adam's ability to inspect Eve that caused him to totally receive her? Certainly not! Don't misunderstand me. I am sure Eve was very attractive to Adam. But since Adam had never seen a woman, he couldn't compare her with anyone else. What, then, was Adam's *basis* for receiving Eve? On what basis was he confident that she was "right" for him? Adam's acceptance of Eve was *based on who God was to him,* not Adam's ability to inspect Eve. God was the One who had created him. *God* created his need. *God* showed Adam his need. And *God* met his need with Eve. *Because Adam trusted God,* he received Eve by faith. He displayed great excitement because of God's *faithfulness,* not because of Eve's performance or lack of performance.

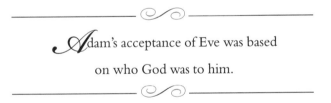

Adam's acceptance of Eve was based on who God was to him.

The point is that only God can meet your needs. He has created a need in you for relationships, which He meets primarily through a mate, but also through the church, family, and friends. He put this need in you to teach you dependence upon Him and to equip you to reflect His image to an imperfect world. You can then reproduce a godly heritage and reign on the earth. He will meet your aloneness need through someone who is also alone and imperfect. Beware of inspecting with your eyes, however. That is the same strategy Satan used to deceive Adam and Eve in Genesis 3.

We are at a key point in God's plan. God sought to protect man from Satan's sin of self-dependence by insuring that he would have to trust God to meet his aloneness needs. Therefore, God *requires that man receive his mate from Him.* If you are single, remember that God desires to provide your needs for a spouse. Wait on Him. God went out of His way to demonstrate the *pattern* of how He would work in history.

HOW TO VIEW
WEAKNESS IN YOUR MATE

Though God meets our needs in His provision of a mate, our mate will not be perfect. (After all, husbands, she's a sinner too! Remember, wives, he will blow it.) Your mate may let you down; at times, your spouse will not meet your expectations. Every spouse certainly has weaknesses. But there is a healthy way to view those weaknesses.

Years ago I viewed Sally's weaknesses as a limitation to me with little hope of ever changing them. The notion of God's meeting my needs through her weaknesses simply made no sense. But God faithfully continued to teach me through His Word, and I began to realize that His perfect provision for my life was Sally—strengths *and* weaknesses. I began asking God for faith to stop seeing her weaknesses as a limitation and instead, to see how those same weaknesses could become a blessing.

With that prayer, I immediately began to experience a new freedom and hope in my marriage. I had relinquished the idea of changing her and simply accepted her by faith as a gift from God. I began to share this truth with others, and as time passed, I realized how great our marriage had become. What changed? God certainly didn't. But as my faith in God grew stronger, my perception of His gift to me in my wife dramatically changed.

What began as a tough step of faith years ago has continued to grow into one of the most blessed realities in my life. Sally might as well be perfect, because God has graciously allowed me to be totally satisfied with her. These truths have released Sally and me to experience hope and enjoyment in our marriage. God continues to reinforce that He has created us specifically for one another. The very things I would have changed in Sally in the beginning have turned out to be the very things I needed to help me mature in Christ.

For example, early in marriage I observed that Sally wasn't very goal-oriented. I'm the opposite. I have always had a five-year plan and a purpose to every plan. On occasion I'd ask, "Don't you have any goals?" She would give me a puzzled look and say, "I don't know. I guess I need to think about that." Sally was, and still is, the type of woman who wakes up every day, and whatever happens, happens.

One of my goals was to prepare for retirement, and at the time, my plan included buying and selling houses. So, during the same time that Sally had our four children in six years, we moved into six different houses. She *never* complained. We just packed up the boxes and moved.

While in the sixth house, it dawned on me what I had been doing to her. The Holy Spirit revealed that the very thing I had been most critical of in her early in our marriage had become a blessing to me. I was now glad she had not changed. The lights went on for me, and I began to thank God for this special woman in my life. *A goal-oriented wife would have never put up with my plans!* Sally made every move fun for the whole family. The friends we have established in every city through her have remained lifelong friends. She is God's gift to me —a fact God continues to reinforce in me each year. In faith, my challenge all along was to simply receive the gift God had prepared for me. Through her I have learned to be more flexible. She, on the other hand, enjoys my goals.

---

*W*hat you view as a weakness

in your mate today may indeed become

a great blessing later in marriage.

Taking this step of faith opened our eyes to the right way of viewing weaknesses in each other. You will find these five truths helpful in regarding your spouse's weaknesses.

1. God will meet your aloneness needs in spite of your mate's weaknesses.

2. God's only agent for changing your mate with promised results is unconditional love. That is also true for any relationship.

3. God actually uses your mate's weaknesses as a tool to perfect your character.

4. Your mate's weaknesses are an opportunity for you to be needed in his or her life.

5. What you view as a weakness in your mate today may indeed become a great blessing later in marriage.

Can you trust God to accomplish this work in your life now through your mate? If you're not yet married, can you trust Him for your future mate? If you can't, don't get married. If you are married and inspecting instead of believing God, then your mate is certainly living under a yoke of performance. Ask God to forgive you. In faith receive your mate from God just as he or she is, and thank Him for meeting your needs through this special person.

You can see how essential having a Christ-centered marriage is. Accepting the weaknesses of your mate in faith only makes sense if you are first able to trust God. Rejecting your mate after marriage is simply doubting God and His provision in your life. Doubt calls God's motives into question, leaving you unable to reflect His glory, reproduce a godly heritage, or reign victoriously in life.

I believe that God gave my wife to me, not because she is perfect, but because God is. Will you by faith receive your mate from God as His perfect provision for you?

A FORMULA FOR MARITAL ONENESS:
Leave Plus Cleave Equals One Flesh

God concluded the Genesis 2 passage by stating another principle for every married couple. This principle reveals the formula for marital oneness. For those who follow it, God promises blessings. The formula is found in verses 24–25: "Therefore shall a man leave his father and his mother, and shall cleave unto his wife: and they shall be one flesh. And they were both naked, the man and his wife, and were not ashamed" (KJV).

Because neither Adam nor Eve had a literal father and mother, we know God introduced in these verses a principle intended for every married couple. The first part of this formula is *leave*. The word *leave* means to "abandon" or "break dependence upon." While no one should dishonor his or her parents, becoming married means breaking one's dependence on them. In fact, this principle would include severing any lingering strings to a former lifestyle: being single, sports, a job, finances, and so on. Countless couples get off to a rocky start due to an unwillingness to assume total responsibility for their new household. Obviously these aspects of life continue after marriage, but they must become secondary to the most important human relationship on earth: the marriage.

The second element in God's formula for marital oneness is found in the word *cleave*: "and shall cleave unto his wife." The word *cleave* means to "stick like glue." This same imagery was used in biblical days to describe melting metals together to form a stronger alloy. Faith in God is required to cleave. Our part is to leave, and God's part is to cleave us together. To the extent that both mates trust God for the outcome of their marriage, both will have the faith to "stick like glue."

Jesus Christ reinforced the application of this principle to all marriages when He said, "Have ye not read, that he which made them at the beginning made them male and female, and said, For this cause shall a man leave father and mother, and shall cleave to his wife; and [the two] shall be one flesh? Wherefore they are no more [two], but one flesh. What therefore God hath joined together, let no man put asunder" (Matthew 19:4–6 KJV).

Every marriage problem stems from either a failure to leave or a failure to cleave.

Clearly, God has established this principle as the basis of marriage. To experience marriage successfully, each mate must 100 percent leave his or her former state and then 100 percent cleave to the mate. We have found in counseling that every marriage problem stems from either a failure to *leave* or a failure to *cleave*. The only way you can 100 percent commit to your mate is to trust God for the outcome. Before marital oneness can occur, both mates must exhibit faith, a step that eliminates the concept of a fifty-fifty relationship.

The third aspect of God's formula for marital oneness is *becoming one flesh*. Here is a wonderful result and blessing of oneness: "They shall be one flesh" (Genesis 2:24 KJV). Loving one's mate by faith, instead of pressing the person to perform, releases amazing blessing and transparency. When God's Word says, "And the man and his wife were both naked and were not ashamed," (verse 25), the word *naked* implies being totally exposed, yet without threat: physically, emotionally, spiritually, or intellectually. Adam and Eve experienced total openness and transparency, with no masks. They were able to become one spiritually, emotionally, and physically. Oneness (one flesh) is the result of marital faith.

With the advent of sin, natural oneness was destroyed. It can be recaptured only through faith in God, and by applying His principles of marriage. Every person has the need to be loved unconditionally. However, that will not happen here on earth unless someone chooses to love you by faith.

If you were formerly divorced or not a Christian when you married, or just aren't positive you're married to the right person, the principle of oneness still works for you. Scripture tells us that God hates divorce (Malachi 2:16), and He desires for you to remain married. Therefore, the principles of leaving, cleaving, and becoming one flesh still represent God's desire for your marriage. If you will leave and cleave by faith, God indicates that oneness will result!

We also know that God forgives past failures when they are confessed to Him (1 John 1:9). He gives us a new beginning and tells us not to look back. Regardless of your past, God's plan for marriage still works today. Don't let Satan confuse you or rob you of a wonderfully satisfying marriage. Become one, and move ahead to reflect God, reproduce, and reign by His power. God is honored each time a couple commits to His plan for marriage.

The couple who believes that God brought them together, and that He will meet their needs in spite of their mate's weaknesses, will experience oneness. We must choose to follow Adam's example of receiving Eve in faith.

SIX

Power in Oneness Through the Holy Spirit

Apart from receiving Jesus Christ as Savior, no other more practical issue exists than understanding the role of the Holy Spirit in marriage. Yet most believers do not understand the ministry and the power of the Holy Spirit: who He is, what He does, or how to release His power in their lives. The result is much confusion concerning His work in our lives.

Power to live the Christian life comes from the Holy Spirit. According to Jesus Himself, the Holy Spirit brings unity between individuals and leads us to love one another in order to honor the Father and the Son, (John 13:34–35; 16:13–14). The Spirit is the key source of oneness in marriage. It's one thing to know the right thing to do —to seek harmony in marriage; it's another matter for husband and wife to do it.

The apostle Paul prayed for believers that God "would grant you, according to the riches of His glory, to be strengthened with power through His Spirit in the inner man" (Ephesians 3:16). Nothing is more important to your marital peace, to the harmony between your spouse and you, than releasing God's power in your marriage. To remain uninformed about the Holy Spirit is equivalent to choosing to fail. For that reason, we need to understand the identity of the Holy Spirit, His attributes, and how He ministers in our lives. By asking the questions "Who?" "What?" and "How?", we can learn much about the Holy Spirit.

WHO IS THE HOLY SPIRIT?

Who exactly is the Holy Spirit? Notice that He is a *who,* not a *what.* Above all, the Holy Spirit is God. The Holy Spirit is the third person of the Trinity: the Father, the Son, and the Holy Spirit. The Scripture itself refers to the Holy Spirit as God (2 Corinthians 3:17–18).

Since He is God, the Holy Spirit possesses divine attributes: He is eternal, all-knowing, all-powerful, and is present everywhere (1 Corinthians 2:10–11; Genesis 1:2; Psalm 139:7–8). Yet the Holy Spirit is distinct from the Father and the Son. Scripture reveals that the only unpardonable sin occurs against the Holy Spirit: rejecting His convictions regarding the work of Christ at the Cross. Clearly, the Holy Spirit is God.

In addition to His divine attributes, the Holy Spirit possesses a personality that includes emotions. Scripture actually portrays a vital relationship between the Holy Spirit and mankind—including you and me—in which we can obey or disobey Him (Acts 5:3). We are warned, "Do not grieve the Holy Spirit of God, by whom you were sealed for the day of redemption" (Ephesians 4:30), and "Do not quench the Spirit" (1 Thessalonians 5:19). Act 7:51 reveals that people can resist the work of the Holy Spirit. Yet, the Holy Spirit desires an intimate relationship with each of us.

At the close of his second letter to the Corinthians, Paul signed off this way, "The grace of the Lord Jesus Christ, and the love of God, and the fellowship of the Holy Spirit, be with you all" (2 Corinthians 13:14). The Holy Spirit deeply desires to be involved in your marriage. Do you desire fellowship with Him? Do you know what that means and what fellowship with Him is like? He has many roles in helping you to ecperience life to the fullest, both personally and with your spouse.

WHAT DOES THE HOLY SPIRIT DO?

The many roles of the Spirit in our lives and marriages are so important that Jesus emphasized the Spirit's significance and many roles while on earth. In His final discourse (John 14–16), Christ repeatedly drew attention to the Holy Spirit's vital role in living the Christian life after His departure.

> "If you love Me, you will keep My commandments. I will ask the Father, and He will give you another Helper, that He may be with you forever; that is the Spirit of truth, whom the world cannot receive, because it does not see Him or know Him, but you know Him because He abides with you and will be in you. I will not leave you as orphans; I will come to you." (John 14:15–18)

> "But I tell you the truth, it is to your advantage that I go away; for if I do not go away, the Helper will not come to you; but if I go, I will send Him to you. But when He, the Spirit of truth, comes, He will guide you into all the truth; for He will not speak on His own initiative, but whatever He hears, He will speak; and He will disclose to you what is to come. He will glorify Me; for He will take of Mine and will disclose it to you." (John 16:7,13–14)

These statements were made at a key transition point in God's eternal plan. Christ was preparing momentarily to finish His role as Savior. Jesus made it clear that after His death, the Holy Spirit would be God's provision for living the Christian life.

Among the Spirit's many roles, let's look at six.

First, the Holy Spirit *convicts and sustains us.* Clearly, the Holy Spirit's influence in our lives begins before we become Christians. While we were yet lost, the Holy Spirit convicted us of sin. Jesus told His disciples, "And He, when He comes, will convict the world concerning sin and righteousness and judgment" (John 16:8). The Holy Spirit enlightens us with the story of Christ, then regenerates our soul with new life in Christ (Titus 3:4–6). Finally, God puts His seal on us for all eternity (Ephesians 1:13, 4:30). Is that important to you and your marriage? Absolutely! The Holy Spirit continues to convict and enlighten us throughout our lives. Marital oneness is dependent on His continued renewal in these vital ministries.

Second, the Holy Spirit *helps us.* In Scripture, He is called *the Helper.* Two points stand out. Notice that Christ said the Father "will give you another Helper, that He may be with you forever" (John 14:16). Some translations use the word "Comforter." The word means to "come alongside and strengthen." Christ was signifying that the Holy Spirit would fill His own place, doing for the disciples what He had done for them while He was on earth.

How important is the Holy Spirit's help to us? Christ indicated that "it is to your advantage that I go away; for if I do not go away, the Helper will not come to you" (John 16:7). Christ recognized that His leaving would bring salvation and the vital ministry of the Holy Spirit. The coming of the Holy Spirit was second in importance only to Christ's glorious and completed work at the Cross. Therefore, just as believers honor the work of Christ, they should also honor the work of the Holy Spirit. Because the Holy Spirit is God, He is worthy to be sought after, worshiped, and praised. The Holy Spirit brings honor to God the Father and God the Son.

----------— ⁓ —----------

*F*aith is trusting God to accomplish

what He says in spite of our mate's weaknesses.

----------— ⁓ —----------

If we desire to succeed in the Christian life, then Christ tells us that His Helper should become a major part of our lives. To become one in marriage, both mates must understand and accept the work of the Holy Spirit. They must cooperate with His plan through daily fellowship with Him.

Third, the Holy Spirit *teaches us.* Christ said it this way: "But the Helper, the Holy Spirit, whom the Father will send in My name, He will teach you all things, and bring to your remembrance all that I said to you" (John 14:26).

As our teacher, the Holy Spirit gives us spiritual knowledge and faith through the Word of God. In the initial chapters of this book, we have talked about developing a faith relationship in marriage instead of a performance-based relationship. A faith relationship can be defined as one in which the participants look beyond their mate's performance to God's sovereignty and promises. Instead of focusing on our mate's weaknesses, which is natural, we instead believe God's Word concerning our marriage. Faith is trusting God to accomplish what He says in spite of our mate's weaknesses. Scripture tells us where faith comes from: "So faith comes from hearing, and hearing by the word of Christ" (Romans 10:17). Where do we find the words of Christ? The Bible, of course.

If you want to be one in your marriage, faith will be required. Faith requires your involvement in studying the Word of Christ. The One who illuminates the Word is the Holy Spirit. "For to us God revealed them through the Spirit; for the Spirit searches all things, even the depths of God. For who among men knows the thoughts of a man except the spirit of the man which is in him? Even so the thoughts of God no one knows except the Spirit of God" (1 Corinthians 2:10–11).

You may have wondered why we have included so many Scripture texts in this book. It's because Sally and I felt both hope and conviction when we read passages like Genesis 1:26–28 and 2:18–25. If your life and marriage are touched by them, it will be the Holy Spirit teaching you. Sally or Don Meredith cannot do that. The Holy Spirit is our instructor, imparting spiritual knowledge and faith through the Word of God.

One of the greatest indications that

I am not depending on the Holy Spirit

is the absence of power in my life.

Fourth, the Holy Spirit *provides us with power.* He grants power to witness, overcome sin, and serve Him, as well as the power to be one in marriage. When Christ commissioned the disciples, He said, "But you will receive power when the Holy Spirit has come upon you;

and you shall be My witnesses both in Jerusalem, and in all Judea and Samaria, and even to the remotest part of the earth" (Acts 1:8).

If you do not experience much power in your life and marriage, faith is the missing ingredient. Why? Because Christ left this earth in order for the Holy Spirit to indwell believers. All we have to do is call upon His power. One of the greatest indications that I am not depending on the Holy Spirit is the absence of power in my life. I cannot overcome my critical spirit in my marriage without His power. I cannot be a testimony to my wife, or anyone else for that matter, if I don't have His power. As a couple, you must be energized by His power to be a witness for Christ in marriage.

Fifth, the Holy Spirit *leads us,* guiding our decisions. Nearly sixty years on Earth has taught Sally and me that life has many twists and turns. Sometimes we anguish in our desires to follow God's leading. As we respond to Him, we draw tremendous comfort from yet another ministry of the Holy Spirit. He promises to provide guidance in life. The apostle Paul wrote, "So then, brethren, we are under obligation, not to the flesh, to live according to the flesh—for if you are living according to the flesh, you must die; but if by the Spirit you are putting to death the deeds of the body, you will live. For all who are being led by the Spirit of God, these are sons of God" (Romans 8:12–14). Clearly, Paul exhorts us to be led by the Spirit.

We love the way Ezekiel describes this leading of the Holy Spirit toward the nation of Israel. "Moreover, I will give you a new heart and put a new spirit within you; and I will remove the heart of stone from your flesh and give you a heart of flesh. I will put My Spirit within you and cause you to walk in My statutes, and you will be careful to observe My ordinances" (Ezekiel 36:26–27). That's precisely what we need in our marriages—the Holy Spirit to take away our stubborn and hardened hearts and cause us to be soft and pliable in His hands. Marital oneness will never happen unless both mates earnestly beseech the Holy Spirit to lead them. "But when He, the Spirit of truth, comes, He will guide you into all the truth" (John 16:13). His will be done, not ours. We will never be one by *our* wills, but only through seeking and following His will.

The final ministry of the Holy Spirit is one many of us desperately need. The Holy Spirit *comforts us.* Four times Jesus referred to the Holy Spirit as the Comforter. While mentioning suffering, Paul said this: "Blessed be the God and Father of our Lord Jesus Christ, the Father of mercies and God of all comfort; who comforts us in all our affliction, so that we will be able to comfort those who are in any affliction with the comfort with which we ourselves are comforted by God" (2 Corinthians 1:3–4).

Life is full of disappointments and afflictions. Sometimes our dreams shatter and our visions go unfulfilled. I, personally, have been burdened with deep discouragement at times. I thank God for the Holy Spirit's comfort. Many times He comforts me through my wife, and vice versa. The Holy Spirit replenishes our souls and reminds us of truth that may not be immediately evident. In His divine power, He replaces fear with hope. He imparts peace instead of despair. At times, this ministry alone sustains us.

What does the Holy Spirit do? He is our sustainer in life. As we release our will to His, He gives perspective and hope. As the psalmist said, "Come, let us worship and bow down, let us kneel before the Lord our Maker" (Psalm 95:6). Often, just kneeling down before the Lord as husband and wife, acknowledging Him as Lord and Creator, brings hope to weary souls. God, the Holy Spirit, brings comfort in the passages of life and marriage.

HOW DO WE RELEASE
THE HOLY SPIRIT'S POWER IN OUR LIVES?

Experiencing the full power of the Holy Spirit is not something we necessarily do. Rather, releasing His power is a deliberate act that we ask *Him* to do in and through us. Allowing Him free reign in our lives can be measured by the fruit He produces in our lives. The Holy Spirit supplies the power; we simply act on His power by faith. The Scripture calls this faith-interaction with the Holy Spirit "fellowship," a time to "walk by the Spirit" (2 Corinthians 13:14; Galatians 5:16).

In order to adequately release the power of the Holy Spirit, we must acknowledge that our lives belong to Him. This includes our past, our present, and our future. All things must be given to Him to use as He desires. The apostle Paul called Christians to make a total sacrifice of their selves:

Therefore I urge you, brethren, by the mercies of God, to present your bodies a living and holy sacrifice, acceptable to God, which is your spiritual service of worship. And do not be conformed to this world, but be transformed by the renewing of your mind, so that you may prove what the will of God is, that which is good and acceptable and perfect. (Romans 12:1–2)

If God created us, He also knows what is best for us at all times. Therefore, it is our *reasonable* service to give Him not only our lives, but everything He entrusts to us. He then will show us that His will is good (for us), acceptable (to us), and perfect (in us).

----------------- ⟡ -----------------

*T*he two prerequisites to

enjoying fellowship with the Holy Spirit

[are] *confession* and *walking by the Spirit.*

----------------- ⟡ -----------------

Are you willing to give up your rights, pride, and willfulness? Can you trust God and His Word? To experience His power requires our total trust in Him.

Releasing the Holy Spirit's power in our lives comes by a faith interaction that leads to fellowship. How do we experience this fellowship? The first epistle of John introduces us to the two prerequisites for enjoying fellowship with the Holy Spirit: *confession* and *walking by the Spirit*. The apostle wrote:

This is the message we have heard from Him and announce to you, that God is Light, and in Him there is no darkness at all. If we say that we have fellowship with Him and yet walk in the darkness, we lie and do not practice the truth; but if we walk in the Light as He Himself is in the Light, we have fellowship with one another, and the blood of Jesus His Son cleanses us from all sin. . . . If we confess our sins, He is faithful and righteous to forgive us our sins and to cleanse us from all unrighteousness. (1 John 1:5–7, 9)

John said that we must submit to God's perspective, or will, if we want to walk in fellowship with Him. He uses light as a metaphor for God's holiness and purity.

Apart from the cross of Christ, no one can claim to be holy. Instead, by faith we must enter into the grace and forgiveness of God shown at the Cross, and thus submit our wills to His control. If we submit to following Him, the Holy Spirit graciously fellowships with us while continually cleansing us from our sin through the blood of the Cross.

Releasing the Holy Spirit's power in our lives includes turning from our selfish attitudes. Confession of sin means agreeing with God that what we did was indeed sin. We then turn from our sin (repent) and ask for God's forgiveness. His power is released as we ask the Holy Spirit to live in us, love through us, and forgive others through us. The Spirit does what is *natural* to Him—living the Christian life. But, now *He lives His life through us.*

This is critical to understand, since we are not "trying" to live the Christian life in our power. Instead, we relinquish our will to the Holy Spirit and trust Him to live through us. This process of trusting, not struggling, should be continual and lifelong. This means a sacrificial life, a cleansed life, and a life filled with power. What a freeing experience!

Paul called this leading of the Holy Spirit "walking by the Spirit," and this second prerequisite for fellowship prevents us from following our selfish desires. As the apostle wrote to the Galatian church,

> Walk by the Spirit, and you will not carry out the desire of the flesh. For the flesh sets its desire against the Spirit, and the Spirit against the flesh; for these are in opposition to one another, so that you may not do the things that you please. But if you are led by the Spirit, you are not under the Law. (Galatians 5:16–18)

Notice that Paul referred to a struggle that occurs in believers' lives: "For the flesh sets its desire against the Spirit, and the Spirit against the flesh; for these are in opposition to one another." *The flesh* is a term describing the natural self-centeredness present in all people, including Christians. These old patterns and tendencies constantly contend with the Holy Spirit for control. When we become Christians, we don't lose our flesh with its desires. The Holy Spirit is the only One who can *control* the flesh—self-centeredness, insensitivity to others, pride, greed, and so on. Under the control of His Spirit, Scripture tells us that the flesh is dead, or powerless.

THE FLESH VERSUS THE SPIRIT

The fruit evident in our lives reveals whether the flesh or the Holy Spirit is in control of our lives. Paul identifies the fruit of the flesh by saying, "Now the deeds of the flesh are evident, which are: immorality, impurity, sensuality, idolatry, sorcery, enmities, strife, jealousy, outbursts of anger, disputes, dissentions, factions, envying, drunkenness, carousing, and things like these, of which I forewarn you, just as I have forewarned you, that those who practice such things will not inherit the kingdom of God" (Galatians 5:19–21).

The first thing we check when couples enter our counseling room is their fruit. If their fruit reveals arguing, jealousy, outbursts of anger, and so on, we know they are not in fellowship with the Holy Spirit. Oneness in marriage is impossible in the flesh.

---

*C*ouples controlled by the Holy Spirit

naturally produce the fruit of the Holy Spirit.

Oneness is a natural by-product.

The fruit of the Holy Spirit contrasts sharply with the fruit of the flesh. "The fruit of the Spirit is love, joy, peace, patience, kindness, goodness, faithfulness, gentleness, self-control" (Galatians 5:22–23). Notice, this is the fruit of His Spirit, not something we create on our own. Christians do not possess these wonderful virtues in and of themselves. We exhibit them because Christ lives in us. Couples controlled by the Holy Spirit naturally produce the fruit of the Holy Spirit. Oneness is a natural by-product. Peace reigns in their homes.

The unity exhibited in marriage is an example to others of their submission to God's Holy Spirit.

Paul reveals that each of us can *choose* who controls our lives. "Now those who belong to Christ Jesus have crucified the flesh with its passions and desires. If we live by the Spirit, let us also walk by the Spirit. Let us not become boastful, challenging one another, envying one another" (Galatians 5:24–26). Because we have become Christians, we no longer are bound by our selfish tendencies. We can choose, by faith, to let the Holy Spirit take over.

THE ROLE OF FAITH

Releasing the Holy Spirit in your life and marriage involves faith and will; and, the apostle Paul says, it involves the power of Christ Himself: "I have been crucified with Christ; and it is no longer I who live, but Christ lives in me; and the life which I now live in the flesh I live by faith in the Son of God, who loved me and gave Himself up for me" (Galatians 2:20).

Walking in the Spirit simply means seeking a deeper, closer walk with the Spirit. The more He has of your life, the more fruit the Spirit can manifest through you. Walking in the Spirit starts with believing that Christ crucified the power of sin in your life by His death on the Cross. *That takes faith.* Next, believe the Holy Spirit will do what the Scriptures say: "If by the Spirit you are putting to death the deeds of the body, you will live. For all who are being led by the Spirit of God, these are sons of God" (Romans 8:13–14).

In the same way—by faith—Christ called His disciples to activate the Holy Spirit. "But you will receive power when the Holy Spirit has come upon you; and you shall be My witnesses both in Jerusalem, and in all Judea and Samaria, and even to the remotest part of the earth" (Acts 1:8). The disciples waited many days, until Pentecost, for the Spirit to come, but they waited in faith. (See Acts 1:12–14; 2:1–4.) Christ asks you to also show faith. It's true that you need help even to believe, but helping is a ministry of the Holy Spirit. He is your Helper, and He will lead you into incredible works for God if you will let Him. The question is, will you take Him at His word? If so, the Holy Spirit's power will be released in your life and marriage. As He convicts you of sin, agree with Him that the behavior or attitude is wrong. Following His lead, ask for forgiveness, and seek His will. Then He is free to exhibit the fruit of the Spirit through your life.

The Holy Spirit gives you the power to be one in marriage, to reflect God's image to a lost world, to reproduce His image through children and disciples, and to rule this world to His glory. The message is clear; the challenge is precise. What you allow the Holy Spirit to do through you will determine the health of your marriage.

How to
Change
Your Mate

Take this quick quiz. God chooses to use two of the following three forces to change behavior in marriage. Which one of the following three approaches does God *not honor?*

1. Loving your spouse unconditionally

2. Giving kindness when you want to retaliate

3. Actively seeking to change your spouse through pouting, intimidation, or manipulation

Obviously the third choice fails to bring about healthy change in marriage, although it's the choice used frequently by most couples. *Nowhere in Scripture are we told to change people.* Only God changes people. He has not ordained you as judge, jury, and executioner over your spouse. Yet one of the most common complaints we hear in counseling is the inability to make a partner change to meet one's expectations. The truth is that God uses the *active force* of agape love (see Ephesians 5:22–33), combined with the *reactive force* of blessing (see 1 Peter 3:8–9), to refine people into His image . . . not ours. Since adjustments of expectations and behavior are such a hotbed of conflict in marriage, this chapter will explore how two people *actually change to become one* in a civil and godly manner.

LOVE: THE ACTIVE FORCE

Few things are as aggravating in life as trying to complete a job without having the right tools. Guys, try cutting down a tree with a bow saw instead of a chain saw, or changing the oil in your car without the correct wrenches. Ladies, try vacuuming the carpet with a handheld Dustbuster instead of a vacuum cleaner. Layer upon layer of frustration builds instead of efficiently getting the job done.

In the same way, God mandates that we use His methods to build oneness in marriage. His primary tool is *agape* love. *Agape* is the Greek word for love, specifically an unconditional love. (We will explore its nature in greater depth shortly.) Most husbands and wives, however, build their marriages using a self-centered, "fleshly" love that inevitably leads to frustration. This kind of love says, "I will be nice to you if you do what I want." Unfortunately, if the other person doesn't do what you want, that river of love evaporates into a tiny trickle of effort.

Conditional love disappears when circumstances change. If spouses change from rich to poor, sexy to unsexy, young to old, social to antisocial, athletic to nonathletic, healthy to unhealthy, or any number of other variables, most mates lose what they define as love. Are you building your marriage on this type of shallow, conditional love? Or are you willing to sell out for "the real thing"—loving your spouse with the powerful love of God? To clarify, let's compare and contrast three different levels of love.

THREE LEVELS OF LOVE

The Greek language used in the New Testament describes three specific levels of love.[1] The first level is *eros,* a love that is completely self-centered or self-absorbed. This kind of love accentuates the emotional and physical, with sexual attraction as the primary focus. Eros says, "Me first. I will love you in order to get what I want." Many couples today get married with eros love as their focal point, and do not even realize it! Why are so many marriages ending in divorce? It is because eros love is selfish, not sacrificial and giving. When the spouse's performance lowers, and feelings subside, eros love evaporates.

The second level of love is *philos*. This love involves mutual, tender affection between two people. It implies a "brotherly love," one we often experience in our family of origin, including our brothers and sisters. While eros love is self-centered, philos love is mutually satisfying. It appreciates and respects the other person. It says, "Yes, I love what you do for me, but I also sincerely respect you."

This level of love involves more sacrificial commitment than eros. The overwhelming majority of marriages in America are based on either eros or philos love. The problem with philos love is that when respect is lost, couples tend to revert to eros love, which by itself is undependable.

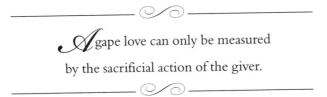

Agape love can only be measured

by the sacrificial action of the giver.

The third level of love is *agape*. Far superior to either of the other two kinds of love, agape is known as God's love. Scripture describes agape as the love that God expressed through His Son Jesus Christ to mankind. This kind of love is the opposite of eros in that it is totally sacrificial. Agape love can only be measured by the sacrificial action of the giver. Unlike eros or philos, agape love does not depend on the attractiveness of the object loved. Rather, *it is defined by the commitment of the giver.* The lover is acting in obedience to God's commandment; therefore this level of love is God directed. It is first an issue between God and man, not between two people, and it does not always run with the natural inclination of feelings. This love is responsible and does not change as feelings change. This is the kind of love verbalized when we say our marriage vows—a never-ending commitment. There are no conditions or performance required for the spouse to receive this ongoing, committed love.

If you are a Christian considering marriage and tell your future mate you love him or her, do you mean eros, philos, or agape love? God never called anyone to marriage apart from agape love. Marital oneness is impossible without it. Since God teaches dependence on Himself in marriage, it is absolutely necessary to trust Him first for this kind of love; then look toward such love developing in you. Agape love is first an issue between God and you. His love will then enable you to love your mate unconditionally by faith.

The Holy Spirit instructs husbands in Ephesians 5:25 to love as Christ loved. How did Christ love? The apostle Peter told us that Christ loved us at the Cross by "entrusting Himself to [His Father]"; this enabled Christ to have the faith to sacrifice for us. Christ remains the ultimate example to us of sacrificial love.

A LIFESTYLE OF LOVE

Biblical (agape) love is best described in 1 Corinthians 13 where the dimensions of love are clearly seen. Those qualities can transform your marriage relationship. Open your Bible and study how five elements of such love can apply to your marriage:

1. *Love is patient.* Genuine agape love will endure an offense even though a tide of emotion is welling up within you demanding retaliation. *Application:* First, such love enables you to have divine patience that waits and prays for the reformation of your mate rather than exhibiting resentment. Second, when you love while suffering patiently, you learn to handle insults and neglect from your mate until God can work through His Word.

2. *Love is not provoked.* Love will not become bitter or resentful as a result of continuous irritation or offenses, or respond to them with touchiness or anger. *Application:* A weakness or offense in your mate will not produce bitterness or anger from you.

3. *Love bears all things.* Love will endure offenses from your mate and throw a cloak of silence over your suffering so that your mate's offenses are not divulged to the world. *Application:* If you have a non-Christian or nonspiritual spouse, be careful not to build a self-righteous attitude in the eyes of others.

While godly church leaders or a few close friends may know your situation, don't make this common knowledge. Indeed, complaining about a spouse to sympathetic ears often becomes the fertile grounds for many affairs. Your mate needs to be able to trust you.

4. *Love believes all things.* Love will choose to believe the best about your mate; it always assumes his or her motives and intentions have integrity. *Application:* Often people become what we convince them they are. If we indicate that we suspect them, they will tend to be untrustworthy. Trusting your mate gives him or her a feeling of self-worth and acceptance, a key to effecting change in your mate.

5. *Love endures all things.* Love has the power to enable you to endure any trial with confidence and patience. Trials produce perseverance and blessings from God. *Application:* Divorce is an indication that you don't endure all things. Agape love doesn't quit when things get tough; it demonstrates permanent commitment.

Studying 1 Corinthians 13:4–8 can be an encouraging marital (or premarital) project. All the verbs in this passage are in the present tense, indicating that these characteristics of love are to be habitual. Because a person does not manifest one of these qualities in every instance, however, does not necessarily signal noncommitment. The apostle Paul is referring to a "lifestyle" of love.

God's love leaves no place for the statement, "I don't love you anymore." It does, however, hold some absolute promises for us. For example, "There is no fear in love; but perfect love casts out fear, because fear involves punishment, and the one who fears is not perfected in love" (1 John 4:18). The word used for love here is *agape.* The verse says two things will result from agape love: (1) Fear will be driven out and (2) love will perfect, or complete, your spouse. Fear is the opposite of faith and hope. If love for your mate depends on performance, he or she will be fearful and insecure. On the other hand, if you love by faith as Christ did, and overlook your mate's weaknesses, your agape love will drive the fear from your mate because there is no retribution. Your mate's peace and satisfaction will then provoke your spouse toward more faith and hope. Usually, your mate will then return the faith love to you.

In addition, God implies that agape love helps perfect the object of your love—your mate. That is, His agape love demonstrated through you will produce faith in your spouse, both toward God and you. How do you change your mate? *You "agape" him or her, and allow God to do the changing.*

If husbands will follow Christ's pattern of love,

they too will . . . have the promise of participating

with Christ in changing their mates.

Another example of the power of *commitment love* occurs in a passage where God ties the promise of Christ's love to marriage. In Ephesians 5:25–33, the husband is charged with the same role in marriage as Christ Himself has with the church. Like Christ, the husband also inherits several promises that Christ received. The Scripture commands husbands to love their wives as Christ loved the church (verse 25), and it reveals (in verses 26–27) two results of Christ's love. First, His love sanctifies us, the church. Second, because of Christ's love, we will be presented back to Him in a perfected state. If husbands will follow Christ's pattern of love, they too will benefit from the same effects that Christ received. They too will have the promise of participating with Christ in changing their mates. Consider these results:

1. When you love your mate as Christ loved, you will sanctify, or set him or her apart by your special commitment. In other words, a woman who is loved unconditionally is set apart from other women who are not loved in this way. A woman who is loved unconditionally is free from marital anxiety and fear and is better able to live a contented life with her spouse and family.

2. A husband who loves with agape love will have the hope of seeing change in his mate. She will be presented back to him, "having no spot or wrinkle or any such thing; but that she would be holy and blameless" (Ephesians 5:27). One day, Christ will show husbands who exhibit such love to their wives how their faith was used to help accomplish these spiritual results. In my life, I have seen God do these things in Sally's life right before my eyes.

In all my years of counseling, I have never seen any other active approach gain these kinds of results. It is not unusual to hear complaints about having to love God's way. *But nothing else works.* Neither manipulation, verbal assault, bribes, nor subtle lying will work like agape love.

Don't experience a poor counterfeit of God's love. Experience agape love toward your mate, and trust God for the outcome. The fearlessness, transparency, and peace of such a relationship are what married life was meant to be. Bless your mate by giving your partner the assurance that he or she will never hear you say, "I don't love you anymore."

BLESSING: THE REACTIVE FORCE OF LOVE

"In the three years since my husband started his new business, the children and I have not had a vacation. We have done without a lot of things so Bob could succeed. Then two weeks ago his real appreciation for us came through loud and clear." Vicki's voice showed anger, and her eyes flashed as she told me her story. "First of all, I got the Master Card bill and discovered that Bob had purchased a used motorboat to the tune of $5,000. When I called him at the office, he exploded and told me that he and some of his buddies were planning to go fishing for ten days in Mexico and needed a boat! I was so furious I hardly spoke to him for the next two weeks.

"The day he left to fish, I took the Visa card and the children and flew home to Mom's for ten days of fun, to the tune of $5,250."

Vicki had done the human thing. She retaliated and "really showed him." But how did it help her? Did it change Bob? Did two wrongs make a right? Was Bob more in love with her than before? Did it serve any useful purpose to have two people insulted instead of one? Three months later Vicki returned for counseling with Bob at her side. The hurt, bitterness, and ruin were still flaming.

Couples today are not prepared for the consequences that result from the insult cycle in their marriages. Yet, many end up as victims. As time passes, these cycles become vicious whirlwinds. Scripture tells us that we can stop these insult cycles by returning a blessing when wronged or insulted.

Our human nature does not want to offer a blessing after receiving an insult. Our instinct is to follow Vicki's example: "I'll show him. He hasn't seen anything yet! I've just begun to fight." In our rights-oriented society, God's way seems ridiculous and painfully slow. We don't think it will work. Rather, we want change instantly because we live in an instant society. Remember, God's ways are not always our ways and His timing is not ours either. What's happening in your marriage? Are you ready to listen to God?

To better understand what God means when He says to return a blessing when insulted, we need to define what the Scripture refers to as an insult and a blessing. There are many examples of each, and we will look at several.

Concerning *insults,* the Scriptures give many exhortations. Seven are particularly relevant to marriage:

1. Name-calling. God admonishes us not to belittle others. Name-calling is always a threat to marital love and causes fear in the one receiving the insult. Any consistent negative reference to someone is demoralizing and destroys self-confidence. (See Matthew 5:22.) Imagine hearing words like *dummy, stupid, moron,* or *idiot* or worse.

2. Sarcasm and ridicule. Dwelling on intellectual, social, or physical ineptness certainly hampers marital oneness. Examples: "You burned the food again!" "Why are you so quiet when we're with our friends? I wish you'd just speak up!" "You can't do anything right!" (See Proverbs 18:6; Ephesians 4:29.)

3. A nagging wife. Scripture is bold in its condemnation of a woman who doesn't trust or respect her husband enough to stop nagging on any given subject. "How many times do I

have to tell you?" or "You *never* do this for me," or "You *always* come home late!" (See Proverbs 21:9; 27:15–16.)

4. A contentious man. Scripture speaks just as forcefully of a quarrelsome man who is always picking a fight. This kind of macho man thinks he is always right, refuses to back down, bullies his wife, and is too arrogant to ask for forgiveness (Proverbs 26:21).

5. An unbridled tongue. Scripture speaks of the powerfully negative effect of the tongue when it is not controlled. We can poison and destroy another person by using profanity, cutting remarks that put down each other, and always citing the negative in any situation. Sometimes the effects can scar our mate or child for life. (See James 3:5–10.)

6. Lying to your spouse. Scripture speaks of the serious consequences of not telling the full truth, covering the truth, or using little white lies. This results in a lack of trust and openness between spouses and causes disunity. "Lying lips are an abomination to the Lord" (Proverbs 12:22).

7. Insult and abuse in general. Immorality (which would include adultery, homosexuality, and pornography), sorcery, enmities (including profanity), strife, dissensions, drunkenness, and unrighteousness of all types are grouped in this last category. (See Galatians 5:19–21.)

When you are wronged, God says to bless a person instead of insulting him. An insult is usually the natural human response, while blessing a person requires a decision of the will and empowerment by the Holy Spirit. Consider the following uses of blessing in Scripture, and apply them to your marriage.

1. Giving praise to God. (See Luke 1:64; 6:28; and 2 Timothy 1:3–6.) Concerning your mate, ask yourself, *What positive qualities about my mate can I use to verbally praise him or her?*

2. Giving thanks to God for His gifts and favor. (See Luke 1:64; 2:28–32; and Mark 6:41.) Concerning your mate, ask yourself,

What qualities about my mate am I thankful for, and how can I communicate this to him or her?

3. Calling down God's favor. (See 1 Samuel 12:23.) Concerning your mate, ask yourself, *What specific areas of my mate's life should I pray that the Lord will bless?*

4. Benefits bestowed. (See Mark 6:41 and Luke 11:13.) Consider benefits (such as gifts, acts of service) that you can bestow upon your mate.

5. Seeking counsel. (See Proverbs 27:9.) Honor your spouse by seeking his or her advice.

6. Encouragement and fellowship. (See Philippians 2:1–4.) Consider areas of your spouse's life where you can encourage him or her. Ask yourself, *Am I spending enough quality time so I know what is really on his or her heart?*

You know what blesses and what insults your mate. If you don't, simply *ask* your mate. These examples from Scripture are mentioned to broaden your perspective. Become an expert on how to bless your spouse, and then practice giving blessings. Remember, "Give, and it will be given to you. They will pour into your lap a good measure—pressed down, shaken together, and running over. For by *your* standard of measure it will be measured to you in return" (Luke 6:38, italics added). If you are always critical, criticism will come back to you. If you are an encourager, encouragement will come back to you. It is *your* choice. Give agape love and it will be returned.

As figure 4 shows, the blessing cycle is as rewarding and ongoing as the insult cycle is damaging and ongoing. And the results could not be more different. The couple caught in the insult cycle find themselves (1) unable to be one in their marriage; (2) unable to reflect, reproduce, and reign; and (3) unable to receive a blessing. In contrast, the couple who enter the blessing cycle find their relationship blessed with (1) oneness; (2) the ability to reflect, reproduce, and reign; and (3) more blessings.

With such great rewards from blessing each other, why do marriages turn into insult battlefields instead of blessings, as God intended? The answer takes us right back to a key biblical theme found

Figure 4
The Cycles of Insults and Blessings

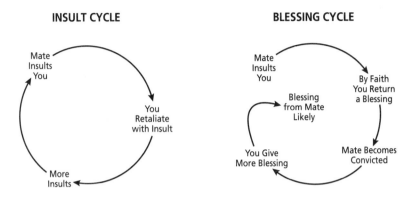

throughout Scripture and highlighted in Galatians 5:16–26. If you are a Christian, two forces are operating in your life. One is your self-centered will (the flesh). The other is your "new spiritual creation" given to you at the point you received Christ as Savior (note 2 Corinthians 5:17). These two are in conflict with one another. Your will follows the natural impulses of the flesh, while your new spiritual creation heeds God's will, as revealed by the Holy Spirit. The Spirit uses Scripture to reveal God's will. These two forces approach life from entirely different perspectives.

The chart on page 99 compares this divergent thought. As you study it, you may be amazed at the difference between God's perspective and man's. God says it this way, "For My thoughts are not your thoughts, neither are your ways My ways" (Isaiah 55:8). The insights on the following page demonstrate the conflicts between the way men and women naturally think compared to God's perspective.

I don't know about you, but when I read through the chart, the Holy Spirit nudges me. "Don, wake up to My ways." The term "faith relationship" demands dependence on God's perspective, not my own. Humanly speaking, it does not make sense for me to bless when I have been wronged. Yet, as the Holy Spirit applies God's perspective through His Word, I begin to think, "Wait a minute, maybe God has a better way!"

The next question we must ask is, "Does God ever give you the right to retaliate?" No, He does not. He does tell us to seek wise counsel. He does give specific instruction concerning church discipline. He does tell us not to be drawn into sin. But He never gives us the right to retaliate. Instead, the New Testament asks that we seek to return good for evil done to us: "Bless those who curse you, pray for those who mistreat you," Jesus said (Luke 6:28); "See that no one repays another with evil for evil, but always seek after that which is good for one another and for all people," Paul added (1 Thessalonians 5:15).

WHY RETURN A BLESSING?

No question about it, God condemns revenge—all the time! With that established, it is wise to look at God's better way. After instructing husbands and wives concerning the marriage relationship (1 Peter 3:1–7), Peter explained why it's better to return a blessing rather than an insult when wronged.

> To sum up, all of you be harmonious, sympathetic, brotherly, kind-hearted, and humble in spirit; not returning evil for evil, or insult for insult, but giving a blessing instead; for you were called for the very purpose that you might inherit a blessing. For "The one who desires life, to love and see good days, must keep his tongue from evil and his lips from speaking deceit. He must turn away from evil and do good; he must seek peace and pursue it. For the eyes of the Lord are toward the righteous, and His ears attend to their prayer, but the face of the Lord is against those who do evil." (1 Peter 3:8–12)

The apostle offered four reasons to give a blessing to those who wrong us. First, Peter said, "for you were called for the very purpose that you might inherit a blessing." In other words, *a blessing beget a blessing.* And a blessing is what God desires for you. He doesn't want you to insult, because He knows that will result in a returned insult, leading to more frustration.

MAN'S PERSPECTIVE VERSUS GOD'S PERSPECTIVE

Man's Perspective (The World's System)	God's Perspective
1. People are my problem.	"Seek first His kingdom and His righteousness, and all these things will be added to you" (Matthew 6:33).
2. Success is the first priority.	For our struggle is not against flesh and blood, but against the . . . powers, against the . . . spiritual forces of wickedness in the heavenly places (Ephesians 6:12).
3. Hold on to what you've got at all costs or you will lose everything.	"Give, and it will be given to you. They will pour into your lap a good measure—pressed down, shaken together, and running over" (Luke 6:38).
4. Material possessions will bring more happiness.	"Blessed are those who hunger and thirst for righteousness, for they shall be satisfied" (Matthew 5:6).
5. Most of my problems are caused by the one in authority.	Every person is to be in subjection to the governing authorities. For there is no authority except from God, and those which exist are established by God. For rulers are not a cause of fear for good behavior, but for evil (Romans 13:1, 3).
6. Love your friends, but get your enemies before they get you.	"But I say to you, love your enemies and pray for those who persecute you" (Matthew 5:44).
7. If only I had married someone more gifted I would be happier.	But one and the same Spirit works all these things, distributing to each one individually just as He wills (1 Corinthians 12:11).
8. In this life, you've got to take care of Old Number One.	"If anyone wants to be first, he shall be last of all and servant of all" (Mark 9:35).
9. My mate can't do anything. If only I had married someone God can use.	I planted, Apollos watered, but God was causing the growth. So then neither the one who plants nor the one who waters is anything, but God who causes the growth (1 Corinthians 3:6–7).
10. I'll teach him or her not to cross me.	Never take your own revenge, beloved, but leave room for the wrath of God, for it is written, "Vengeance is Mine, I will repay," says the Lord (Romans 12:19).
11. I'm going to the top and I don't care whom I have to step on to get there.	Humble yourselves under the mighty hand of God, that He may exalt you at the proper time (1 Peter 5:6).

Second, God implies that blessing one another will result in "good days," or a long life. Certainly, that is true. Stress destroys, while *blessing prospers and benefits.*

Third, when you bless, you have the hope of pleasing God, and that "His ears attend to [your] prayers." That is a significant promise. When we are in God's will, "all authority in heaven and earth" is available. *Returning a blessing allows God to bless us through answered prayer.*

*W*hy return a blessing?

Because it works!

Finally, God further releases you from the need to return an insult by saying in effect, "If your mate is really wrong, I will take care of it." The Scripture declares, "The face of the Lord is against those who do evil." *God can better deal with your mate* because of His great love and forgiveness that tempers His justice. When God disciplines, He redeems. When you try to play God in your mate's life, you destroy.

Which makes sense to you now, returning a blessing or an insult? His Word indicates that returning a blessing is God's will. It opens the door to blessing, life, good days, and God's favor. So why return a blessing? Because it works!

The next question is, "How do we give a blessing?" Christ's own life provides an excellent example as described in 1 Peter 2:21–25. The context is suffering in trials, yet a wonderful picture emerges showing how Christ responded to insults. Think back to Vicki's response to Bob and compare her actions to our Lord's response. Do you see the difference?

HOW TO RESPOND TO INSULTS

Our model for how to respond to insults is the Master Himself, the Lord Jesus Christ. Peter has described how the Lord Jesus responded to insults.

For you have been called for this purpose, since Christ also suffered for you, leaving you an example for you to follow in His steps, who committed no sin, nor was any deceit found in His mouth; and while being reviled, He did not revile in return; while suffering, He uttered no threats, but kept entrusting Himself to Him who judges righteously; and He Himself bore our sins in His body on the cross, so that we might die to sin and live to righteousness; for by His wounds you were healed. (1 Peter 2:21–24)

The first thing we are to do is *remove any sin in our own lives.* Note that Christ was innocent—He had committed no sin! When your mate insults you, first ask yourself, "Did I do anything to provoke my mate?" If you did, confess your sin, first to God, and then to your mate. Usually we bear some fault too. Perhaps 90 percent of the time when Sally insults me, I did something to provoke her. My first step —your first step—in responding to your mate's insult is to determine your role in her response. "Sweetheart, I know I must have done something to provoke your response. How have I hurt you? Can we talk about it?"

After understanding the issue, you may need to ask your mate's forgiveness. Only when you confess *your* failure will God be able to work in your mate's life, either to bring conviction or restoration.

The second step in responding to an insult is to return a blessing. Christ died to heal the very people who had ignored Him, wounded Him, and crucified Him. The implication is clear: Christ not only refused to insult them, but He blessed them. Each mate must make a *willful* decision to return a blessing in spite of the hurt just experienced. Your will must be submitted to God's will. Look beneath the insult to the reason for the behavior or words. Look for ways to bless your mate. Look for ways to praise your mate and communicate your love deliberately. Do something specific to build up his or her spirit.

Most people insult others because they are hurting inside, and have tremendous emotional needs themselves. Insulting can be a re- lease mechanism. You can interrupt this tendency with kindness. Je- sus uttered no threats when insults were thrown at Him. He had every "right" to threaten the people who were sending Him to the cross. But Jesus knew that insults and threats do not work. They only cause more hatred. By not returning an insult, you humble yourself and allow God's principle of blessing to work.

The third step is just as important: *Commit yourself and your situation to the Lord.* Jesus turned to His Father for hope, insight, and strength. Humanly, Christ did not want to suffer, but He kept His Father's perspective. He knew that even though it was momentarily tough, in the long run His Father's will was best. You must yield to God's will and perspective also.

As you yield to the Holy Spirit, He will change your perspective. You will begin to say, "God gave me this person, and therefore *my struggle is not against my mate,* but Satan, who deceives me into thinking that my mate is the problem." That is the source of all spiritual problems, according to Ephesians 6:12. As you catch God's perspective, you can thank Him for the situation. As you yield the situation to the Lord, it can be used to make you more like Christ. Only the Lord can convict and adequately deal with your mate's offense.

The last step is: *Be willing to suffer in order that God can heal your offender.* Jesus *purposed* to die on a cross so that you might be healed (1 Peter 2:24–25). God never says the momentary cost of returning a blessing will be small. In fact, He implies that at times it will be very tough. (Remember, the Crucifixion was an ugly event.) Yet, God guarantees a blessing for your efforts and peace in your heart. It may not be just what you expect, but God will bless you in ways you have never dreamed.

Determine to stop the insult cycle and return a blessing instead through the power of the Holy Spirit. The more you learn to bless, the more blessings you will receive in return.

How do you change your mate? You apply the active force of agape love. When wronged, apply the reactive force of love which is the act of blessing. Both of these go against our human nature. That is why faith is necessary. Faith occurs when you override your human instinct by acting on God's Word, through the power of the Holy Spirit.

NOTE

1. These definitions of love are found in William E. Vine, *Vine's Expository Dictionary of New Testament Words* (Uhrichsville, Ohio: Barbour, 1985).

EIGHT

Love and Submission

$\mathscr{F}$rom its founding in 1776, in a war of independence against England, America and its people have always valued independence and self-reliance. And now, at the start of the twenty-first century, the thought of yielding a measure of autonomy or space in order to submit to anyone still contradicts every cultural message Americans hear. Many husbands and wives feel the same way: "I don't want to lose my independence to my spouse." Yet in the Bible's call to serve each other, the Scriptures teach husbands and wives to practice submission to each other.

Years ago, a deeply agitated woman came to us with her concerns regarding her role as wife. She thought she knew what God intended for women, but told us, "I have struggled with guilt feelings lately because I've begun to question the issue of submission in marriage for a woman. I am confused about what submission means and if it applies to women anymore."

Men are equally confused. Some see a wife's submission as the opportunity to become a macho, rude dictator, bellowing out commands. Christian couples with marital problems often admit they're confused about biblical roles. When Sally and I began to analyze this frustration over the issue of headship and submission, we found several questions at the crux of the debate:

- Did God create men and women equally?

- Did God intend for men and women to have different roles in the family?

- Do men have an advantage over women from God's perspective?

These issues have reached great magnitude because of our cultural emphasis on the "oppressed" wife. To answer these questions, let's begin with the scriptural job descriptions of men and women in marriage. The man's responsibility is stated in Ephesians 5:25–33 and 1 Peter 3:7, and the woman's responsibility is found in 1 Peter 3:1–6. Both responsibilities, however, are summed up in Ephesians 5:21: "Be subject to one another in the fear of Christ."

As you approach these Scriptures and consider these points, be careful. You may soon begin thinking, *Oh, not that again! If I hear these points one more time, I'll scream!* If these issues are not placed in the larger context of God's whole plan for marriage, they can become legalistic. From God's perspective, however, love and submission should not be a source of struggle nor a task to accomplish. Rather, such submission can be the evidence of a loving relationship.

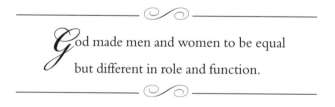

God made men and women to be equal but different in role and function.

We will define biblically what love and submission mean. The accompanying chart on God's perspective on these words summarizes well the differences in the husbands' and wives' roles.

GOD'S PERSPECTIVE ON
LOVE AND SUBMISSION

	Husband	**Wife**
Key Verse (Ephesians 5:21)	"Be subject to one another in the fear of Christ."	"Be subject to one another in the fear of Christ."
Role	Love	Submission
Absolute Command	*Love* without conditions	*Submit* without a word
Supporting Scriptures	Ephesians 5:25–33; 1 Peter 3:7	1 Peter 2:13; 3:1–6
Promises	1. Sanctify her 2. Present her 3. Have prayers answered	1. Silence foolishness 2. May win husband to Christ 3. Have no fear 4. Have a spirit precious to God
Pictures	1. Love her as own body 2. Nourish her 3. Cherish her 4. Honor/understand her 5. Exemplify Christ	1. Gentle and quiet spirit 2. Respect husband 3. Holy women who hoped in God 4. The example of Sarah

Although the roles of husband and wife differ, a careful review of Ephesians 5:25–33 and 1 Peter 2:13; 3:1–7 demonstrates that *there is no favoritism on God's part toward either the man or the woman.* In fact, the two passages are parallel in several important ways. (See chart above.) As we look at the Ephesians and 1 Peter passages, one fundamental truth becomes clear: God made men and women to be equal but different in role and function.

Each passage begins with an absolute command that is very strong in the original language. They leave little doubt about the responsibilities of both the husband and wife. Each passage lists a number of exciting promises that result from following the commands. These promises motivate, soften, and become the hope of the commands. The passages also include illustrations to clarify our understanding of each role and to provide a hint as to how you can fulfill them successfully.

We also need to consider the similar contexts in which these two passages are written. In Ephesians 1–3, Paul wrote that Christians are to walk in a manner worthy of His calling because of Christ's suffering at the Cross. In Ephesians 5:15–21, he added that as we walk in the Spirit of God, four things will result.

1. We will speak to one another with psalms and hymns (understanding God's motivation).

2. We will sing and make melody with our hearts to the Lord (praise Him for that motivation).

3. We will be able to give thanks for all things in His name (because we understand His will).

4. We'll make ourselves subject to one another in the fear of the Lord (because we understand God's provisions for relationships).

For a husband, he will understand Christ's challenge only when he understands how to walk in the power of the Holy Spirit and seeks the mind of Christ. Without that perspective, a man will never fulfill his role. With that perspective, a husband can understand what it means to submit to his wife, and what it means to love his wife. He will learn, for instance, that submission means listening to her heart, respecting her opinions, and honoring her thoughts.

In like manner, before teaching the importance of a wife's submission in 1 Peter 3, Peter drew the readers' minds back to Christ's suffering on the cross. There Jesus submitted Himself to unjust suffering, and "kept entrusting Himself to Him [God the Father] who judges righteously" (2:23). Peter was saying, "Women, before you can properly understand your responsibility to your husbands, you too must have the perspective of Christ." So, the contexts of both passages are parallel in that both focus on Christ's suffering prior to the call to obedience.

THE ABSOLUTE COMMANDS

As you compare the two passages, look at the absolute command to each mate. First, read the command to the man: "Husbands, love your wives, just as Christ also loved the church and gave Himself up for her" (Ephesians 5:25). The word for *love* used in this command is the word *agape,* which you will recall is a God-given and God-directed love that does not exist apart from God. We called it "commitment love" in the previous chapter. That is why it is illustrated by Christ's love for the church.

What was the church doing when Christ came and died for her? She was nonexistent. (The few followers, called "disciples," were in despair and disarray after Jesus' arrest.) People were rebelling against God and ultimately crucified Jesus Christ! By Christ's example, we learn that God's love was initiated totally by the Giver; it did not take into account the actions of the one loved (Romans 5:8). The same must be true as husbands love their wives. Husbands are to love sacrificially while setting aside their rights, pleasing God the Father just as Christ did.

Now men, read the command of Ephesians 5:25 again. Talk about 100 percent responsibility! There are no exception clauses here. There are no excuses. Should God ask you one day, "How did you love your wife?" you might be tempted to say, "Well, Lord, You know I loved her in certain areas. But it was hard to love her completely. She didn't always deserve it. And remember, Lord, she had an affair, and she was untrustworthy. I just couldn't love her unconditionally." You might try to prove she didn't deserve your love.

But the Lord will say, "I didn't ask you about your mate's weaknesses. I asked you, 'How did you respond to My command to love her as I loved you?'"

There are no exceptions! God knows your mate's weaknesses, because He created her. He even knows her sins, because Christ died for her. He wants you to love her, no matter what she does or does not do. That is your 100 percent responsibility! Hard? Indeed, it's impossible on your own. But by His Spirit working in and through you, you can love your wife as Jesus Christ loved us and gave Himself up for us.

Submission means that you place yourself

under another. . . . It is *never* the right of the

husband to make his wife submit.

The wife, on the other hand, is given an equally firm command. "In the same way, you wives, be submissive to your own husbands so that even if any of them are disobedient to the word, they may be won without a word by the behavior of their wives, as they observe your chaste and respectful behavior" (1 Peter 3:1–2). Just as Christ was submissive to the Cross, wives are called upon to submit to their husbands. The word *submission* is a very strong word in the Greek language. It was a military term, meaning literally, "to place oneself under another." Notice, submission means that you place yourself under another; it is 100 percent your responsibility. It is *never* the right of the husband to make his wife submit. His only right is to love her and serve her, demonstrating Christ's attitude toward the church. Christ placed Himself under His Father, which resulted in His death on the cross. This kind of submission is not based on emotion but upon the very character and example of God.

Submission in marriage means "respecting your husband enough to follow his leadership in the home." A synonym for submission is respect. Ephesians 5:33 says, "The wife must see to it that she respects her husband."

Women are to submit themselves to their husbands as they entrust themselves to God. Again, the wife, like the husband, will have to answer the Lord when He asks, "How did you respond with respect to your husband?" No matter how strong the proof of her husband's weaknesses, there are no exception clauses in God's command to her. Peter made this clear by stating, "even if any of them are disobedient to the word." Then Peter sealed the strength of the command by saying a wife must submit to her husband's leadership with a respectful attitude. It takes tremendous spiritual perspective to submit as Christ did, yet He requires it of godly wives. Certainly it's easier to follow a man who loves the Lord and is being obedient to love his wife unconditionally.

We see no favoritism in these parallel commands to the husband or wife. Both are overwhelming commands. Both require complete submission to Jesus Christ. Both husband and wife must willingly obey under the loving care of a mighty God! Be careful not to inject your cultural thinking at this point. When you submit to your mate, you are submitting to God. He is not talking about winners and losers. Instead, God outlines His will for marriage that results in oneness. Trust Him that when He commands us to love and submit, He intends only blessing and unity.

PROMISES TO HUSBANDS ABOUT WIVES

The Lord is gracious to quickly draw our eyes from these strong commands to the associated promises. Our obedience brings positive outcomes. First, the husband draws encouragement from the results of showing love similar to Christ's: "That He might sanctify her, having cleansed her by the washing of water with the word, that He might present to Himself the church in all her glory, having no spot or wrinkle or any such thing; but that she should be holy and blameless" (Ephesians 5:26–27).

The promise to the husband is twofold: (1) that he might sanctify his wife and (2) that he might present his wife spotless. A husband cannot accomplish these things in the eternal sense as God does, but this kind of love on the man's part will produce results similar to those coming from Christ's love.

The word *sanctify* should encourage us. *Sanctify* means to "set apart from the rest." You're set apart in Christ in that you're free from death because of His death and resurrection. A wife is set apart by her husband because his love is not based on her performance, and she is therefore free to be "more than ordinary."

Just as the Spirit reminds us daily of our forgiveness by washing us with the Word of God, so a wife, through experience, must be able to trust her husband's commitment to love her. And, men, this seemingly impossible command to love is not so hard when you realize the results will be a receptive and appreciative wife! A woman who is loved with agape love is a pleasant and beautiful woman indeed!

Next, God promises the husband that if he loves his wife sacrificially, she will be perfected by this love. When Paul speaks of having "no spot or wrinkle," the word *spot* means "moral stain," and the word *wrinkle* means to be "filled with inner struggles." Using these words implies the outward and inner results of Christ's work. Christ's work results in eternal perfection, but Paul implies the similar, temporal result of the husband's sacrificial love. Christ's love is so freeing and creative in your life that you're able to experience both outward joy and inward peace. The face and countenance of a Christian should not show the signs of inward stress and pressure that an unbeliever may have.

During my married life, God has graciously demonstrated the "no spot or wrinkle" promise to me. Sally has always desired to please God with all her heart. But I also believe Sally has become a godly wife and mother, partially because I have dared to love her unconditionally by faith. When I place her under performance, fear results. Yet, when I love her as Christ loved the church, hope and faith are the results. Sacrificial love produces a more beautiful wife, internally as well as externally.

---

*O*ur [wives will] actually love God more . . .

because God's love has had "arms" through [us].

Husbands, I am not saying that God will make our wives "beauties" right before our eyes. But our wives will find inner joy by having loving relationships with us. Sally does not spend even minutes a day being distressed over our relationship. My commitment love has freed her to become characterized by an outward glow and an inner joy that makes her very attractive. I am convinced that one day God will show me that my faith was used by Him to make her more internally peaceful, which showed on her countenance. Added to that is a change that she has expressed to others and me. Sally actually loves God more, and understands the unconditional love of God better, because God's love has had "arms" through me.

God promises husbands that if they can keep Christ's perspective in loving their wives, He will actually use husbands as instruments of redemption in the lives of their mates. Her peace and joy will be noticeable. People will say, "What a joy it is to know your wife. Her life really motivates me."

God gives another powerful promise to husbands: "You husbands in the same way, live with your wives in an understanding way, as with someone weaker, since she is a woman; and show her honor as a fellow heir of the grace of life, so that your prayers will not be hindered" (1 Peter 3:7). If husbands will honor their wives as joint heirs with them in the grace of life, God will answer their prayers. Understanding her will involve a great deal of time and energy. It involves *asking* her how she feels on any given subject and not always trying to solve her problems. Sometimes she doesn't need a solution, just a listening ear. She needs to feel that you *want* to understand her.

What does it mean to honor your wife? It simply means to consider your wife's needs above your own. Honoring means listening to her and communicating with her. It involves giving her quality time and attention. If you value your wife's insights concerning life, marriage, raising children, friendships, careers, church, decision making, how your gifts differ, and so on, she will truly be a joint heir with you. There will be harmony, not discord. Sin will not be obstructing your relationship with God, and God promises answers to your prayers!

Husbands, you cannot demand respect from your wife; you can only earn it. You do this through tenderly and patiently understanding and honoring her. This is what it means to be "subject to one another in the fear of Christ" (Ephesians 5:21).

PROMISES TO WIVES ABOUT HUSBANDS

Likewise, the woman also has been given promises that result from her submission to her husband. Respectful submission is always voluntary on her part. It requires faith in God's perspective and plan. Peter described the promises in his first epistle:

> For such is the will of God that by doing right you may silence the ignorance of foolish men. . . . Your adornment must not be merely external—braiding the hair, and wearing gold jewelry, or putting on dresses; but let it be the hidden person of the heart, with the imperishable quality of a gentle and quiet spirit, which is precious in the sight of God. For in this way in former times the holy women also, who hoped in God, used to adorn themselves, being submissive to their own husbands; just as Sarah obeyed Abraham, calling him lord, and you have become her children if you do what is right without being frightened by any fear. (1 Peter 2:15; 3:3–6)

God instructs women to submit to their husbands, not because of their perfection, but because of God's faithfulness. A woman should never regard submission as being to her husband, but as being to the Lord. God's faithfulness is your hope, just as it was the hope of Christ as He went to the Cross.

The first promise occurs in 1 Peter 2:15. While not yet speaking directly of marriage, Peter mentions a result of submission that occurs from a relationship other than marriage. Peter tells us that if we do what is right, we can "silence the ignorance of foolish men." That is powerful.

This is followed closely by a second promise, indicated in 1 Peter 3:1. Wives who submit themselves as unto the Lord may win their husbands by their behavior without nagging. Again, God shows the wife that she can be an instrument of the Lord, effecting change in his attitude toward God. Notice, there is no other way to effect change in a husband. Nagging is neither a way of making peace nor of making a husband do what is right. The woman who struggles with submission has never really believed God that her respect is the key to his response. Her resistance only leads to frustration for both of them.

Wives, we're not talking about poor communication here. Throughout Scripture you find instruction on how and when to communicate. However, this passage deals with weakness on the part of the husband. When a wife nears the point of nagging or preaching, she must get out of the way so that God can work in her husband's life. This is a tough decision requiring faith and complete dependence on God.

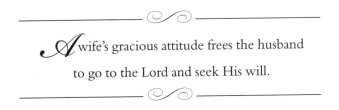

A wife's gracious attitude frees the husband to go to the Lord and seek His will.

I have grown to so respect my wife that when I am wrong and she is gracious toward me, I feel overwhelmed and confess my mistakes. She may say something like, "Don, I have expressed my opinion on that subject, but I want you to pray about it. Before the Lord, whatever you decide, we will do." As a man, I can bear witness to the power God releases in my life through her gracious attitude. When she does that, I want to do right! I always pray about decisions, especially when she has first expressed her feelings. I listen to her much more effectively when I feel that she is not judging me or mistrusting me. I have often found that her intuition has kept me from making a mistake that I would have made if I hadn't consulted her.

A wife's gracious attitude frees the husband to go to the Lord and seek His will. The couple can then pray about it together, and God will always show them what to do.

Finally, God promises that the woman who keeps His perspective and trusts Him more than human devices (trickery, manipulative words, or physical charms) will be precious to God. What a promise! God places a very high value on a woman who esteems her husband. He says her trust will cause her to have a "gentle and quiet spirit." *Gentle* means not causing her husband to be frustrated or ruffled. *Quiet* means causing her husband to be soothed when he is upset or frustrated. A mother is naturally good at this with children but not always with her husband.

To the woman who seeks God's heart, it means a great deal to be precious in His sight. Peter wrote that respectful wives would be like Sarah, who had no fear. Most women are paralyzed with fears: fears of growing old, losing love, appreciation, or wealth, facing death, and more. Most would love to be fearless. God chose Sarah to illustrate

His promise. Her husband Abraham was far from perfect. Yet Sarah submitted herself and was not afraid. A very wealthy man, Abraham was called by God to leave his home in search of a new place. God promised to lead him. Abraham went by faith, taking Sarah and all their servants. During the trip, Abraham came upon a very harsh kingdom. Rather than trusting God that he wouldn't be killed, he told Sarah to pretend to be his sister. She would find favor with the king and thus spare Abraham's life. And Sarah remained silent!

Let me ask you: Has your husband ever told you to do anything so ridiculous—to pretend you are his sister? Abraham pulled this trick, not once, but twice! Sarah's hope was not in Abraham at this point, but in God, who judges righteously. God protected her both times. And God can protect you from your husband's mistakes even when you are affected by them. If you are faithful, God will give you peace and richly bless your path.

Considering both the commands and promises to the husband and wife, there is no advantage to either role. Both commands call for total faith. On the other hand, God's promises to both husbands and wives take the sting out of the commands and give hope.

HIS TO CHERISH, HERS TO TRUST

The New Testament explains how these roles are implemented. Husbands are to cherish; wives are to trust. The husband receives two practical word pictures of his role: the words *cherish* and *nourish*. Here's how the apostle Paul pictured the husband loving his wife: "So husbands ought also to love their own wives as their own bodies. He who loves his own wife loves himself; for no one ever hated his own flesh, but nourishes and cherishes it, just as Christ also does the church, because we are members of His body" (Ephesians 5:28–30).

Husbands are to love their wives as they love their own bodies. Most men are instinctively aware of the value of their own bodies; they do not have to consciously think about loving them. If anyone, or anything, hurts or threatens it, they respond with corrective action. God is telling us men how important our wives should be. You and I are to be so sensitive to our wives that if anything hurt or threatened them, we would take immediate corrective action to protect them.

You are to *nourish* and *cherish* your wife. These two words are beautiful ways of describing the love God is talking about. *Nourish,* used only twice in the New Testament, literally means "to keep warm at the perfect temperature." It was used to describe a mother bird keeping her chicks under her wing at perfect body temperature. Husbands are to be so involved in their wives' care that they know from moment to moment what her needs are in order to meet them.

Even more descriptive is the word *cherish.* The only other place this word is used in Scripture is 1 Thessalonians 2:7: "But we proved to be gentle among you, as a nursing mother tenderly cares for her own children." Have you ever noticed that mothers are almost perfect in responding to the needs of their newborn? Even women who normally struggle when serving others usually have a natural desire to give joyfully to their babies without resentment. An infant makes selfish demands with little capacity to appreciate its mother's sacrifice. Yet a good mother will reshape her life for her baby with very little struggle. She does it because she feels blessed, and she senses her absolute responsibility. She has an innate desire to do what has to be done.

A woman who puts her hope in God
instead of in human schemes exhibits a
gentle and quiet spirit toward her husband.

Think of that picture of a loving mother: In spite of her burden, a mother instinctively knows that her baby is a blessing from God.

This illustration opened my eyes to God's perspective. God was telling me that if I really understood how important Sally was to my creation purpose, I would gladly treat her as a mother would treat a nursing newborn. The lights went on. What God said in Genesis 1 and 2 took on an even more beautiful meaning. Like naming the animals for Adam, this passage registered for me. Sally's meaning as a gift and provision deepened tremendously. She became valuable and precious to me.

Men, our culture does not teach us to view marriage this way. Such care and concern for wives are not found in the average American home. Yet this is God's pattern. Do you love your wife as much as you do your own body? Do you know her needs? Are you sensitive to her? Have you altered your lifestyle in order that she might be set apart and glorified? Do you treat her with dignity and honor her? Do you take this responsibility from the Lord as completely as Christ took His responsibility for you, regardless of performance? Are you totally committed to her?

God illustrates submission to wives by talking about their "respectful behavior," their "gentle and quiet spirit," and their "hope in God." Each of these perspectives is dependent upon knowing and trusting God. First, the wife begins by demonstrating a respectful attitude toward her husband. God says, "Love him into right behavior." When your husband is wrong, your first response is usually to tell him so. God says there is a better way—a way that will win him without condemning words. The only way a woman can act respectfully when her husband falters is to view God as the guarantor of her needs. When a wife understands how God made her husband, she will discover from Scripture how to wisely influence him to submit to God.

A woman who puts her hope in God instead of in human schemes exhibits a gentle and quiet spirit toward her husband. Remember, 1 Peter 3 contrasts her outer and inner beauty. Peter wrote that women should not ignore their physical appearance, but to concentrate on the inner qualities. Wives, you do need to look good for your husbands. But your primary efforts are to be in developing your spiritual walk with the Lord, so that Christlike qualities will come through to your husband.

Jesus loves your husband and died for him. Your life should exemplify that. A gentle and quiet spirit will soothe the soul of your husband like nothing else in the world. He will enjoy coming home to you.

The woman who places her hope in God will be able to call her husband "lord." This means she is able to esteem him above what he deserves, because she views him from God's perspective. Her loving spirit toward him then will free him to submit to the Lord and grow spiritually. With proper love and submission, there will be oneness in marriage. The cycle of loving and esteeming is a blessing cycle indeed!

UNDERSTANDING MEN'S AND WOMEN'S ROLES:
The Legalistic Level

In working with Christians, I have discovered three basic levels of understanding of the husband's and wife's roles and responsibilities. These levels are as different as night and day. Evaluate them and decide where you are—and where you need to be.

Many church people live at *the legalistic level*. As husbands and wives, they understand that God commands them to be lovers or submitters. They know these two commands but feel they are impossible to obey. After a talk on "headship and submission," these spouses always try to find a way out. The wife may say, "Please pray for me as I try to submit to this monster that I married." The husband may say, "I'm the head, but she won't do anything I tell her to do." They've both missed the point altogether.

Down through the centuries, men have used the issue of "headship" as a club over their wives' heads. Completely missing their responsibility to love, they hear only the command for their wives to submit. They feel right in "lording it over" their wives. No wonder wives resent their husbands!

― ∾ ―

Some wives . . . think the word submit means

"to be walked on," . . . The concept . . . [has]

no basis whatsoever in Scripture.

― ∾ ―

An equally unfortunate response shown by some wives who object to God's command to submit is to deny the command altogether. Their need to defend their rights reveals a basic legalistic fear that God is going to deny them something. Perhaps they fear that they will not be fulfilled as a person. They think the word *submit* means "to be walked on," or "to become a doormat." These women have missed the bigger picture of Christ's commands. The concepts of "lording it over" and "being walked on" have no basis whatsoever in Scripture. Fear and rebellion result from these misunderstandings.

There is very little hope for the legalistic man and woman. Either defensive or defeated, they run from one book to the next, trying to find the key. One week they might try a new plan and for several weeks their hopes are high. Soon, however, the newness of the project wears off. Things happen to discourage them. Once again, they begin to search for another book or marriage seminar. Books and seminars are fine, but rightly understanding the Word of God, mixed with faith, is what endures!

UNDERSTANDING ROLES:
The Promise Level

The next level of understanding is significantly better. *The promise level* exists when couples look beyond God's command to love and submit to His promise of blessing. Many successful marriages are at this level of understanding because they focus on God's promises. They live with joyful expectancy of God working in their marriages. They believe and act upon God's Word that produces results in their lives and reinforces their efforts. Their marriages grow in hope based on the certainty of God's Word. In and through God's promises, they are assured of everything needed to make life successful.

The potential of a marriage focused on God's promises is clear: "His divine power has granted to us everything pertaining to life and godliness, through the true knowledge of Him who called us by His own glory and excellence. For by these He has granted to us His precious and magnificent promises, so that by them you may become partakers of the divine nature" (2 Peter 1:3–4).

Beyond leaning on God's promises, what could possibly add to your understanding of love and submission? The answer is: seeing life from God's perspective. When we trust that God's perspective on marriage roles is right, we are moving to the wisdom level about our marriages.

UNDERSTANDING ROLES:
The Wisdom Level

Wisdom is the final level of understanding. Wisdom involves living and seeing life from God's perspective. Only through God's wisdom, made known through the Holy Spirit, can you come to fully accept and embrace love and submission. Each mate must individually come to the point of totally rejoicing in his or her roles because they are from God's loving hand. It takes wisdom to do that.

Wisdom is essential. Without it you are still vulnerable. More important, wisdom recognizes the integrity of God's character. Few Christians realize that their questioning of love and submission really questions the character of God. Ask yourself, "How did I come to question God in the first place concerning roles?" We believe the main reason Christians question their roles is that ultimately they do not trust God's good character. They doubt God's plan; they doubt that He designed the best way of relating in marriage. Godly wisdom says our roles were created by a loving God for our benefit.

Several things are vital if Christians desire wisdom. First, you must ask the Holy Spirit to teach you. Second, you need to understand who caused marriage and relational problems in the first place. Originally, who was the author of sin? Satan. How did he deceive Adam and Eve? He lied to them. Who do you think is the source of the world's rejection of God's order in marriage? Yes, Satan. The Father of Lies is still at work. In the next chapter, Satan's schemes will be revealed.

Finally, wisdom flourishes in an atmosphere of mutual submission where each partner serves the other. Servanthood marked the ministry of Christ, and accordingly, God's Word directs husbands and wives to be subject to one another (Ephesians 5:21). A man serves a woman by providing her greatest need: love. A woman serves a man by providing his greatest need: respect.

After understanding Satan and how he deceives people, you must embrace God and His Word. When you establish your trust in Him, and ignore Satan's lies, then you can step out in faith. Wisdom will allow you to set aside your fear (of limitations) in assuming the roles of love and submission. Rightly understanding the Word, revealed to you through the Holy Spirit, releases you from being deceived again. God's promises can be understood and enacted upon more freely. Oneness is then possible, to the praise and honor of God.

NINE

Wisdom

or Deceit

$\mathcal{S}$ometimes a husband becomes frustrated over God's command to love his wife no matter what—even if she has disappointed him a thousand times. At times, he may recoil with, "I don't have to put up with this. She's driving me crazy!" Similarly, a wife may cry "unfair" when she learns that her scriptural responsibility to submit applies even when her husband is insensitive and irresponsible. "It's not fair!" she may say. "I can't respect a man like that."

How can we handle these situations wisely? Love and submission sound great, but regrettably, they are tough issues in real life. In this chapter you will discover why men and women struggle with their marriage roles.

Thus far, you have seen that God is the author of relationships. It was God who created the need in you for relationships, and God who chose to make Adam and Eve His example for marriage. Since God is ultimately responsible to meet our needs, we know that He will not allow anything to prevent Him from meeting these respon-

sibilities. Therefore, God guarantees the outcome of relationships that are directed by Him.

As we learned in the previous chapter, God does not consider either role in marriage as better. God did not create the husband and wife roles to be issues of performance, importance, success, or even superiority. Both are vital to marital blessing. When God told couples to love and submit, He did not intend strife to be the result. Love and submission are simply God's basis for marital oneness. Without love and submission, there can be no oneness. If couples reject God's order, they cannot fulfill His or their purposes in their marriages.

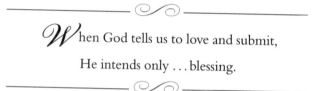

When God tells us to love and submit,

He intends only . . . blessing.

The apostle Paul emphasized the importance of God's order; it applies equally to the Trinity as it does to a married couple: "But I want you to understand that Christ is the head of every man, and the man is the head of a woman, and God is the head of Christ" (1 Corinthians 11:3). Obviously God has created an order for successful relationships. His intention for marriage compares to His relationship with the Trinity. That's good news, for God intends no less for marriage than for Himself. In fact, Christ was both lover and submitter, and saw no threat in either role. He knew that His role, compared to His Father's, had nothing to do with winning or losing. Is Christ any less God than the Father? Any less glorified? Certainly not!

When God tells us to love and submit, He intends only order, blessing, and oneness—not struggle. The problem, then, is not that God made a mistake providing roles, but rather that people have been deceived. A person who sees life from God's perspective, and who understands God's purpose concerning relationships, will not question His order. Husbands and wives controlled by self-centeredness will question any differences between the roles as being unfair.

DECEPTION IN THE GARDEN

Couples must realize that Satan is the source of their confusion concerning love and submission. Satan wants you to see your mate as the problem rather than himself. Yet the Scriptures plainly teach that such marital struggles are spiritual in nature. "For our struggle is not against flesh and blood [people], but against the rulers, against the powers, against the world forces of this darkness, against the spiritual forces of wickedness in the heavenly places" (Ephesians 6:12).

Satan delights in destroying marriages because oneness in marriage is a threat to his purposes. If he can destroy marriages, he can also limit God's purposes for that couple. And his strategy is to feed us lies—lies about our partner and about God's plan. Recall what Jesus said about Satan: "He was a murderer from the beginning, and does not stand in the truth because there is no truth in him. Whenever he speaks a lie, he speaks from his own nature, for he is a liar and the father of lies" (John 8:44). Satan knows that if his lies are successful, he can end oneness on earth.

Look at the example of Satan's deceit in the Garden of Eden in Genesis 3. God created a perfect environment; every need had been met. Adam and Eve had no desire for other things, no longings, no dreams of things being better. Since God desired this perfect relationship to last for eternity, He placed the tree of life within the garden. If Adam and Eve ate from this tree first, they would live for all eternity in a perfect state.

The only threat to this eternal perfection was another tree, the tree of the knowledge of good and evil. God told Adam and Eve not to eat of that tree saying, *"If you eat of it, you will surely die."* Since they had no sinful nature, and since they were perfectly dependent on the Lord, they did not even consider the tree to be a struggle. Adam and Eve trusted God. They knew that not eating from that tree was totally for their good!

However, Satan distorted the purpose of the tree. He disputed God's purpose by calling His Word into question. (See Genesis 3:1–7.) He said they would not die if they ate of the tree, and implied that the real reason God did not want them to eat of the tree was because they would become like God. His message was: "God is really trying to limit you. He is trying to keep you from being like

Him." Satan subtly changed God's purpose from one of protection to one of limitation. Satan appealed to their eyes, appetites, and pride in tempting them. They believed a lie, and they sinned.

Satan is still in the business of deceiving. He uses the same tactics today. When God originally instructed you to love and submit, what was His purpose? It was to allow you to experience relationships, accomplish His plan of the ages, meet your needs, and to equip you to reflect, reproduce, and reign. God knew that without love and submission, there would be no satisfying relationships and no oneness.

Satan has distorted God's purpose by suggesting that love and submission present a limitation, by telling husbands to resist being lovers, and wives to resent submitting. "Why should I love her? She doesn't deserve it." Or "Why should I submit to him? He's no better than I am. I'm smarter, more talented, and more successful." Like in the garden, Satan deceives people into seeing love and submission as limits to rights and freedom in marriage.

GOD'S REDEMPTIVE SOLUTIONS

After Adam and Eve had sinned, God inquired into what they had done. "The man said, 'The woman whom You gave to be with me, she gave me from the tree, and I ate.' Then the Lord God said to the woman, 'What is this you have done?' And the woman said, 'The serpent deceived me, and I ate'" (verses 12–13). What happened to their oneness? Adam immediately blamed Eve by failing to take responsibility. Ultimately, Adam blamed God for giving Eve to him. Adam believed a lie and then blamed God.

Who had changed? Not God! Both Adam and Eve were deceived and disobeyed God. This taste of rebellion gave birth to the self-centeredness of man. Oneness in marriage has suffered since that event.

In love, God has intervened in history to rescue humankind and to defeat Satan's rebellion. First, God established a redemptive curse for Adam and Eve. The woman was given the burden of bearing children and rearing them in the home. "I will greatly multiply your pain in childbirth, in pain you shall bring forth children; yet your desire shall be for your husband, and he shall rule over you" (verse 16).

The man was given the mandate to toil in life for sustenance by hard work: "Cursed is the ground because of you; in toil you shall eat of it all the days of your life. Both thorns and thistles it shall grow for you; and you will eat the plants of the field" (verses 17–18). God greatly increased Adam and Eve's burden to protect them from their selfishness.

Yet God demonstrated His grace by removing Adam and Eve from the garden (verse 23) so that their struggle with sin and death would not be eternal, but temporary. The stage was thereby set for all people to receive new bodies for all eternity by the coming of Christ. God's ultimate act of love—sending His only Son to die on a cross so that men and women could again be in perfect union with Him—will one day bring those who receive the Savior into a perfect environment, with a perfected body and mind. God's response in the garden was a curse. But His gracious and redemptive solution to man's rebellion will someday restore us to the perfect state of Genesis 1 and 2.

Genesis 3:16 contains a statement that has become the source of the current debate on love and submission. God said, "[The man] shall rule over [the woman]." Today, American culture rebels against this statement. However, the word *rule* means to lead and to make decisions. It doesn't imply dictatorship in any way.

------------------- ∽ -------------------

If Christians do not submit themselves to

each other in humility, they will become a threat,

a discouragement . . . in the lives of their mates.

------------------- ∽ -------------------

Prior to the Fall, Adam and Eve's oneness with God and with each other functioned perfectly. Their submission to God was not in question. There was no mention of submission between Adam and Eve because both were totally submitted to God "as one." When sin occurred, Adam and Eve lost their oneness. To protect them from their self-centeredness, God ordained an order of relationships. This order is necessary for oneness and blessing in marriage. Even though

men and women are now confused because of Satan's deceit, God's order remains the same. It takes both love and submission to experience oneness.

After the lie in the garden, Satan's second greatest lie concerns love and submission. When God said to love and submit, He intended only good. Without love and submission, God cannot meet our aloneness needs. Without love and submission, oneness is impossible. Only through oneness can God's purposes be accomplished. Satan does not want that! If Christians do not submit themselves to each other in humility, they will become a threat, a discouragement, and a source of rejection and judgment in the lives of their mates. Unless they love and serve unconditionally, they will never gain respect. There are no agape relationships without both love and submission.

Satan deceives us by appealing to our pride and self-centered nature. He convinces husbands that it is justifiable to demand their wives' obedience, while simultaneously whispering to wives that submission equals oppression. As was stated earlier, those thoughts are antibiblical. Each mate should ask God's forgiveness for doubting His creation of roles in marriage. By faith, accept God's forgiveness and power, and live according to His Word.

In the future, share these truths with others to insure they are renewed in your own life. Only as you renew your mind with Scripture can the Holy Spirit protect you from ignorance and Satan's deceit. Thank God for your new understanding of love and submission. Encourage your mate with your new insight and commitment.

WISDOM:
Having God's Viewpoint

By trusting God the Father, Jesus could view love and submission not as limitations but as the greatest blessings in all eternity. Christ both loved the church and submitted to His Father. Consider His perspective and the result of both roles from the following passage.

> Therefore if there is any encouragement in Christ, if there is any consolation of love, if there is any fellowship of the Spirit, if any affection and compassion, make my joy complete by being of the same mind, maintaining the same love, united in spirit, intent on one pur-

pose. Do nothing from selfishness or empty conceit, but with humility of mind regard one another as more important than yourselves; do not merely look out for your own personal interests, but also for the interests of others. Have this attitude in yourselves which was also in Christ Jesus, who, although He existed in the form of God, did not regard equality with God a thing to be grasped.... He humbled Himself by becoming obedient to the point of death, even death on a cross. For this reason also, God highly exalted Him. (Philippians 2:1–6; 8–9)

The apostle Paul said that if we desire to experience encouragement in Christ, love, fellowship of the Spirit, compassion, or affection in this life, we must be one with others and with God. He described oneness as "being of the same mind, maintaining the same love, united in spirit, intent on one purpose." The goals that Paul mentioned describe desires that are common to all people. Oneness is God's goal for all relationships, be they in the Trinity, the church, or in marriage.

The key to finding oneness, Paul wrote, is having humility of mind toward others. Obviously selfishness has no place here. Many people fear that being humble means being spineless. However, humility is not an emotional cowering, but a mark of one with a strong awareness of God's sovereignty in any given situation. This perspective allows both husbands and wives to esteem each other above themselves. Without a humble attitude, there is no encouragement, love, fellowship, affection, or compassion. With Christ's attitude, however, you can serve your mate freely, without being resentful or feeling limited. Jesus displayed the perfect example while washing His disciples' feet.

> Having loved his own who were in the world, he now showed them the full extent of his love. He poured water into a basin and began to wash his disciples' feet, drying them with the towel that was wrapped around him. "Do you understand what I have done for you?" he asked them. "You call me 'Teacher' and 'Lord,' and rightly so, for that is what I am. Now that I, your Lord and Teacher, have washed your feet, you also should wash one another's feet. I have set you an example that you should do as I have done for you" (John 13:1, 5, 12–15 NIV).

Remember, God created you to be incomplete without relationships. He created you to be unable to accomplish your creation purposes of reflecting His image, reproducing a godly heritage, or reigning on earth without relationships. God cannot meet your needs without love and submission. As you keep God's perspective of relationships before you, His commands to love or submit become not limits but the door to relationships and blessings. Therefore, with a humble attitude, you can actually esteem others higher than yourself, even in tough situations. You can serve others in love. That is how Jesus Christ Himself lived.

His commands to love or submit become

not limits but the door to relationships and blessings.

The call for us, as husbands, is to graciously love and serve our wives, thereby allowing them to become beautiful women of God.

The call for us, as wives, is to graciously esteem our husbands by giving them respect, thereby encouraging them to follow Christ.

Every great marriage has two people who are free from the struggle of questioning God's Word. They recognize that Satan will try to deceive them; thus neither will regard the other mate as the problem. Nor does either mate succumb to Satan's lies. Each knows that he has already been defeated at the Cross. The two mates are victorious over Satan's schemes, claiming the victory that Jesus already won, "having disarmed the powers and authorities, . . . triumphing over them by the cross" (Colossians 2:15 NIV). The result of a couple's faith and obedience will be oneness and blessing in their personal lives and in their marriage.

FIVE VITAL COMMITMENTS

As we conclude part 2 of *Two . . . Becoming One,* consider the faith principles of chapters 4–9 that can allow you to experience a supernatural faith relationship in your marriage. Each of these insights requires faith on your part. As you read through the following list of marriage commitments, ask yourself these two questions: (1) Do I understand what God is saying? (2) Am I applying faith concerning this issue right now?

Each of the following commitments is vital to a faith marriage.

1. Couples need to commit themselves to God's purposes of reflecting, reproducing, and reigning.

2. Couples must accept each other from God as His personal provision for their needs.

3. Couples must release God's power in their marriage by daily submitting to the Holy Spirit.

4. Couples must understand that they can only change their mate through the active force of agape love or the reactive force of blessing.

5. Couples must seek God's wisdom concerning love and submission.

These five commitments form the core of a faith relationship. Nothing is more practical to married life than these. Review these commitments often.

The call for oneness reaches into all relationships, and was part of Jesus' prayer to the Father just before He died: "I do not ask on behalf of these alone, but for those also who believe in Me through their word; that they may all be one; even as You, Father, are in Me and I in You, that they also may be in Us, so that the world may believe that You sent Me" (John 17:20–21). God's plan to reach a lost world would depend on oneness. So marriage success requires oneness.

At this point you may be thinking, "These are great principles, but how do I apply them to the practical areas of marriage, such as communication, money, sex, and so on?" Let me say that these five major commitments are the basis or foundation for the practical areas. If you don't understand the faith concepts just covered, you will not be able to apply faith to the practical areas of marriage. Biblical faith is defined as follows. "Now faith is the assurance of things hoped for, the conviction of things not seen" (Hebrews 11:1).

Many times in marriage, your human instinct will override God's perspective. At those times, ideally, God will bring a Scripture verse to your mind, and faith will take over. Your marriage will then be characterized as one that acts supernaturally, based on the facts of God's Word, not on human ingenuity.

Now we can move on to part 3 and the everyday issues that occur in marriage such as male and female differences, communication, romance, finances, trials, and in-laws. As we keep God's perspective of the principles just covered, the daily areas developed in the next section will fall into place.

PART THREE

*Applying
Biblical Principles
to Your Marriage*

TEN

A Man of Commitment

$\mathcal{W}$hat is the mark of a great husband? Is it financial responsibility, social prominence, strength and vigor, or being a successful father? As important as these areas are, there is a much greater issue. The mark of a great husband is an absolute, unfailing commitment to his wife. A husband cannot bless his wife more than by loving her as a gift from God. Husbands who faithfully ask God for marital direction are rare indeed. As men, we often fail to recognize marriage as a covenant with our mate and with God.

THE MARRIAGE COVENANT

When a man marries, he makes a commitment, or covenant, with God and his wife to (1) oversee his family in order that they might reflect the image of God properly, (2) raise his children to love and follow the Lord, and (3) provide leadership in reigning over what God gives him. As God's man, the husband is to be responsible to God for his wife and family.

Our Lord Jesus talked plainly about a man's marriage covenant:

"So they are no longer two, but one flesh. What therefore God has joined together, let no man separate" (Matthew 19:6). I feel deep fear in my heart when I think of men, especially Christian men, who break this covenant. Divorce is not God's will. It's always a poor solution with tremendous negative ramifications. Below is a vivid description of how God feels about a husband's breaking that marriage vow through divorce.

> The Lord has been a witness between you and the wife of your youth, against whom you have dealt treacherously, though she is your companion and your wife by covenant. But not one has done so who has a remnant of the Spirit. And what did that one do while he was seeking a godly offspring? Take heed then to your spirit, and let no one deal treacherously against the wife of your youth. "For I hate divorce," says the Lord, the God of Israel, "and him who covers his garment with wrong," says the Lord of hosts. "So take heed to your spirit, that you do not deal treacherously." (Malachi 2:14–16)

God Himself is a witness and a participant in the covenant a husband makes with his wife. No man can break that covenant and be led by the Spirit of God. God not only hates divorce, but He will judge the one who does the wrong in the divorce. God considers a man's responsibility toward his wife as a covenant with Him. He gave marriage to man as a blessing; therefore, the husband is responsible to be faithful to that covenant, no matter what the cost. It is much more difficult to raise up godly offspring when there has been a divorce. God not only hates divorce because oneness is destroyed, but because children are irreversibly affected. Oneness is broken in divorce, resulting in great pain to both the couple and the children.

God takes His covenants seriously, and marriage is a covenant. If you want to be characterized as a great husband, put away any thoughts about divorce or finding a better mate. Place your faith in God and commit yourself to sacrificial love that will, over time, soften even the hardest heart.

IF YOU HAVE TO "TOUGH IT OUT"

James offered several instructions about responding to tough trials in James 1:2–7. Later he described godly responses to disagreements.

This you know, my beloved brethren. But everyone must be quick to hear, slow to speak and slow to anger; for the anger of man does not achieve the righteousness of God. Therefore, putting aside all filthiness and all that remains of wickedness, in humility receive the word implanted, which is able to save your souls. But prove yourselves doers of the word, and not merely hearers who delude themselves." (James 1:19–22)

Based on James's advice, here is a helpful list to remember during trying times in marriage. If there is a battle in your marriage, take note of the following:

1. Don't react, but listen to your wife.

2. Don't speak too quickly; wait for your emotions to subside.

3. Don't explode in anger; nothing good ever comes from outbursts of anger.

4. Stop your immoral involvement such as lying, cheating, bad language, pornography, and so on.

5. Seek counsel if any of the above points (1–4) have become negative behavior or habits.

6. Humbly study God's Word for the answers to your problems, seeking counsel when necessary.

7. Act on your faith, not on your feelings.

8. Boldly believe God, regardless of your wife's response. This may include renewing your covenant with your mate.

James 5:16 contains two final points of instruction: "Confess your sins to one another, and pray for one another." Thus, here are items nine and ten:

9. Confess your sins to your wife so both of you can be emotionally healed.

10. Pray earnestly. God has the ability and desire to change your life, motivate your wife, and remove your fears.

The sovereignty of God can motivate us as husbands. Just think: God is a partner with you in your marriage! That should inspire you to serve and please Him. Be aware that your marriage is part of God's eternal plan. You have entered into a marriage covenant, or agreement, and God is a partner with you.

RULE AND SERVE

As I search Scripture to discover God's will for husbands, here are two of the most salient duties: Husbands are to rule and serve.

In the Old Testament, God said, "[The man] shall rule over [the woman]" (Genesis 3:16). In the New Testament, God compared a husband's responsibility to his wife to that of Christ's responsibility to the church (Ephesians 5:25). These truths indicate two major principles in the practice of the husband's covenant to his wife. First, he is to rule. You are a benevolent ruler, not a dictator. Men are to take authority with the humility of a servant. Rather than demanding respect from your wife, you can only earn it. Demanding destroys a wife emotionally, and may eventually destroy the marriage. *Ruling means taking authority with a gracious, loving spirit* toward your wife and children. The goal is the second truth of the covenant: to serve them and encourage them to be all that God wants them to be.

Indeed, the husband moves beyond ruler to be a priest to his wife. The word *priest* means *minister,* emphasizing the role of servant and counselor. You are to be so aware of her needs that you go out of the way to meet them. Most men do not know the needs of their wives without asking them. Don't assume you know until she tells you. Communication is the most important aspect of serving. Serve her, be her loving administrator, and take authority for her life and needs in a way that supports and encourages her.

There must be a careful balance in both of these responsibilities to rule and to be a priest/servant. If the husband overemphasizes his authority, his wife will lose respect and trust. If the husband is only a servant, she will be insecure and lack direction. In searching both Scripture and common sense for what it means to rule (lead) and to be a servant in marriage, we have noticed several specific areas of responsibility for a man. As the husband, he should:

- Protect
- Provide
- Initiate love
- Pray
- Emphasize future hope
- Take authority in conflict
- Meet physical needs

- Support relationship development
- Share time struggles
- Help with children's discipline and instruction
- Communicate, communicate, communicate!

Three major commands are given in the New Testament to husbands describing how to fulfill the responsibilities listed above.

1. Understand Your Wife

Husbands ought to understand, or "know," their wives, wrote the apostle Peter: "You husbands in the same way, live with your wives in an understanding way, as with someone weaker, since she is a woman; and show her honor as a fellow heir of the grace of life, so that your prayers will not be hindered" (1 Peter 3:7). Peter is commanding you to be an expert about your wife.

How ow can you be out of fellowship with your wife

and expect God to answer when you pray?

In order to understand her, you must make it a point to *ask* your wife about her emotional, spiritual, physical, and intellectual needs. Seek your wife's opinion regularly. Knowing her is not an automatic thing. If you don't work at hearing her, you won't know when she is under stress, when she just needs some physical exercise, when she needs a day off, or a night out with you. To understand her also means to honor her, to lift her up, to treat her with utmost respect. The word "weaker vessel" means "fine china." Treat her like fine china, not everyday pottery. She is of great value to you.

Do you know what a perfect day is for your wife? A perfect date? What she really likes to do on vacations? If not, find out. Do you have good communication with her on a daily basis? Peter commanded a husband to know his wife, living with her "in an understanding way"; otherwise sin and struggle will prevail, and a man's prayers will not be answered. How can you be out of fellowship with your wife and expect God to answer when you pray?

"Fellow heirs" means that all of life and all God's blessings are to be shared by the two of you. Decisions you make—raising the children, moving, changing jobs, church, trials, joys and frustrations, and many others—all are to be shared. *Never* make decisions concerning any of these things without complete communication and agreement with your wife.

2. Be Responsible to Your Wife

You must know your wife so completely that you can uniquely apply your responsibilities to fit her specific needs. The Scripture commands that husbands love their wives "just as Christ also loved the church and gave Himself up for her" (Ephesians 5:25). God's command to love includes the idea of giving up your life for her in the same way Christ gave Himself up for the church.

Although husbands do not expect God will require them literally to die, they should be willing. God expects us men to get involved in all issues that cause our wives to fear, physically or emotionally. Physical protection, financial protection, emotional protection, fear of failure, fear of aging, and meeting the spiritual and physical needs of children are good examples of issues where a husband might sacrifice for his wife. The husband shields her from the fear of facing issues alone that may cause her fear or frustration. So as you prepare to meet your wife's needs, first know her and sacrificially take responsibility for her fears and desires.

3. Love Your Wife as You Love Yourself

Paul commanded husbands "to love their own wives as their own bodies" by nourishing and cherishing them (Ephesians 5:28–29). These words connote comfort. Paul is saying to attend sensitively and selflessly to your wife's needs like a mother would a nursing child. Keep her warm by monitoring her intimate emotional and physical needs, just as you care daily for your own needs.

God commands you, in your covenant with Him, to give up your own selfishness by putting her first in priority after Him.

STRATEGIES FOR APPLYING THE COVENANT

Develop a strategy for your wife and family. After you determine the areas of importance in light of your wife's needs, then establish several objectives in each area. Develop a plan for each objective, set priorities, and then schedule their application. A little planning will improve your success significantly.

The following are some ideas from our marriage counseling. Let the Holy Spirit show you which of the following you need to apply to your wife and family.

Leadership

A good husband thrives on being a "shock absorber" for his wife by anticipating his wife's needs and fears. Here are three practical ways to provide leadership for your wife.

First, encourage self-worth. The factors that affect feelings of self-worth are usually obvious: intellect, appearance, productivity, success in relationships, and financial freedom, among others. Discover mutual areas of interest with your wife and work at communication in that area.

Some of the best ways to encourage your wife include seeking out her intellectual interests and finding one where she can teach you. Show interest in her appearance, and support her desire to have a sufficient wardrobe for career and social events. Become an expert on her abilities. If she has a hobby, encourage her. If she does something well in private, sensitively make her friends aware of those skills or qualities. Look for ways to involve her talents publicly. If she is a mother, help her develop in-home income, if she desires it. Assist with household chores and especially be involved in raising your children. Monitor her relationships and assist her in developing friends. Help her organize her schedule. Steps like these help to build her self-worth.

Second, provide comfort. Never allow your wife to experience pain without sharing it with her. A death in the family, a difficult child, frustration in her career, or a disappointment in relationships may require your help. Comfort her and take responsibility for helping her find a solution.

Third, facilitate spiritual maturity. Your hope for mutual faith in your marriage is related to your wife's maturity as well as yours. Do everything possible to assist her spiritual interest. Encourage her efforts to minister to others or attend church functions. As a couple, plan to be involved in leading small groups or teaching Sunday school. Plan activities with your children to free your wife. One of her greatest joys, however, will be watching you take spiritual leadership in your home and church. Many wives have expressed their joy in seeing their husbands excel spiritually.

Financial Security

Work at giving your wife financial hope for the future. A personal savings account for her is important if possible. Special needs like lingerie, hair styling, exercise classes, and hobbies are not all that expensive, and they mean a lot to her. Take family finances seriously. Study chapter 14, apply it to your own situation, and make a personal commitment to adjust according to God's will.

The Scripture strongly advocates that a husband provide for the welfare of his wife. "But if anyone does not provide for his own, and especially for those of his household, he has denied the faith and is worse than an unbeliever" (1 Timothy 5:8).

Romance

Romance in marriage is a man's shared responsibility; romantic moments are extremely important to a woman. Be a romantic lover to your mate. Women love small, inexpensive surprises, small jewelry, flowers purchased from a street vendor—and not just on birthdays or holidays. Unique gifts are great, too. An occasional love letter or card catches her off guard. Quantity is not so important as quality and consistency. (Chapter 13 will provide specific ideas for cultivating romance.)

Romance includes kindling and maintaining sexual interest. And the Scriptures tell a husband to enjoy sexual passion with his wife, and with her alone. "Let your fountain be blessed, and rejoice in the wife of your youth. As a loving hind and a graceful doe, let her breasts satisfy you at all times; be exhilarated always with her love" (Proverbs 5:18–19). Delighting yourself in your wife's physical charms will not only make her feel cherished but will focus your attention on her, where it should be.

Communication

Your wife must communicate with you to maintain her confidence and emotional stability. She cannot respond adequately without a total relationship. Romance will die without communication. If your wife says that you do not communicate with her enough, seek counsel to help define and correct the problem.

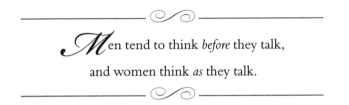

*M*en tend to think *before* they talk,

and women think *as* they talk.

Men and women tend to define communication differently. If a man doesn't look at his wife and listen as she talks (sometimes up to thirty minutes) before giving his opinion, then she feels they have not communicated. Women *need* to talk to solve a problem. Men tend to want the bottom line with fewer words expressed. Men tend to think *before* they talk, and women think *as* they talk. Learn this well.

Husbands, never give your wives the silent treatment. Love requires regular communication. Instead of withholding yourself, open your life to her. Give her words of encouragement. Don't withhold positive words that have the power to heal.

Communication includes talking about feelings of anger. Remember, anger is a common human emotion; you should recognize and deal with it quickly. "Do not let the sun go down on your anger," Paul warned (Ephesians 4:26). Why? Because God knows that when you accumulate anger, it keeps you from putting the past

behind you. Only forgiveness heals the past while renewing your hope for the future.

Be very careful about accumulating unresolved conflict in your marriage. "Do not let any unwholesome talk come out of your mouths, but only what is helpful for building others up according to their needs, that it may benefit those who listen. . . . Be kind and compassionate to one another, forgiving each other, just as in Christ God forgave you" (Ephesians 4:29, 32 NIV).

Hurtful words tend to stay around a long time. Sometimes, after little verbal shots you take at your mate, you may spend a lot of time trying to undo them. Be quick to ask for forgiveness when hurtful things are said. Remember, "It is to a man's honor to avoid strife, but every fool is quick to quarrel" (Proverbs. 20:3 NIV).

Make daily communication with your spouse a priority. Ask her often how you are doing in this important area of marriage and be prepared to work a lifetime improving on this skill. Don't ever take for granted that you are communicating enough. Learn to communicate according to *her* definition.

Prayer

Pray for your wife daily. Ask God to give you love for her and to help you be sensitive to her needs. It's also important to pray for your children on a daily basis. Ask your wife and children how to pray for them. As the years pass, the children will come to you or call you with their prayer requests, even when they leave home.

Open prayer, perhaps more than any other thing, demonstrates your care for them and ultimately shows them God's love.

Authority During Decision Making

Decisions and conflicts constantly develop in the home. Men are to assume authority during such conflicts. Instead of being passive, they are to take responsibility and become involved in the decision making.

If the right decision is not obvious between you and your spouse, take responsibility to insure that the decision is made. If there is conflict between your children, help them resolve it. Husbands and wives need to set examples for their children in conflict resolution. A passive, uninvolved father is especially frustrating to children.

Time Management and Physical Activity

Time management is a major problem for most wives. A husband is in the best position to assist his wife in working out her schedule and priorities. Begin by working out a priority list with your wife. General categories that need to be considered are personal time with the Lord, marriage relationship, relationships with children, career, friendships, church ministry, recreation, and work.

Set a brief planning meeting, perhaps fifteen minutes each Sunday night, to agree on a week's schedule. Help her eliminate activities that leave her overcommitted. After understanding her schedule, help her diversify activities. Arrange for her to be out of the home regularly if you have small children. When possible, commit to staying home to give her that freedom. Taking care of your children when your wife is away is not baby-sitting. It is your responsibility as a joint heir in the grace of life.

A balanced schedule includes specific time together alone, even if you have children. A date once a week will do wonders for both of you and will strengthen your communication. Take charge on Friday night and let her sleep in on Saturday morning. If she has preschoolers, relieve her from the five o'clock horror show at dinner and the bedtime scene by taking over with one or both duties. If your wife works outside the home, make sure that you share the chores and the responsibilities of the home with her. *Ask* her what needs to be done.

With your wife's and your busy schedules, take an active interest in your wife's and your health. Exercise together if possible, and make sure you both have physical checkups. Convince your wife that her body is attractive. Do not let her set unrealistic weight goals. A husband's sensitivity, coupled with realistic weight goals, will result in your wife's satisfaction with her body. Allow her to share her concerns about your physical situation, also. Don't reject her input.

Taking walks together frequently can also help your communication. If possible, discover a mutually enjoyable sport such as tennis, golf, fishing, bicycling, or running.

The Family's Identity and Hope

Help your wife and children understand that they are part of a uniquely developed family by God's choice. Develop this identity with activities that promote family togetherness, such as vacations, sports, church activities, youth activities, or family camps. If you promote family times as the children grow up, they will return for family outings even as adults. Make it a priority.

As part of securing your family's identity, always communicate your future vision and plans with your wife. Get her full input. Nothing affects a woman more than low expectations for your future, and that of your children. Don't expect your wife to understand your future vision without explaining it to her and making sure she comprehends it. If you plan to make a career change, she should not be the last one to find out about it.

Mutual Interests

Too many couples lose their desire to be together because they no longer have mutual interests. If you try, you can develop some mutual interests. Travel is a great possibility. Fun, sports, hobbies, and intellectual stimulation are all vital to a growing relationship.

Aging

Without spiritual interest, productivity, relationships, and responsibilities, people really suffer as they age. Protect yourselves from slow depression; develop spiritual interests and activities that can continue until death. If you do find depression developing, seek godly advice or medical help.

Typically, our wives will begin to dream about their future goals during their forties. The empty nest is right around the corner, and your wife will want to know that the rest of her life will be productive. Her early dreams are usually wrapped up in marriage and raising children. But, along about early midlife, she begins to ask questions about what *she* wants to accomplish as she ages. Help your wife fulfill her dreams. Many women begin second careers at this point.

When grandchildren appear, husbands should allow those youngsters to become part of their lives, even if the grandchildren seem to scramble your schedule and exhaust you. They can help you stay active and make you feel important.

Continue to work as long as possible before retiring and then use your talents part time. Earlier sacrifices of making time for ministry will pay off in your later years. As your work-related activities decrease, your service to the Lord and His people can continually increase. Most of all, maintain your commitment to your wife intellectually, emotionally, spiritually, and sexually.

CHILD REARING

For those couples who have children, a key strategy involves rearing children. By sharing the pressure of raising the children, husbands protect and honor their wives in a very practical way. The children's educational and emotional needs as well as their physical and spiritual development are vital to a mother's feeling of well-being. Husbands should seek to understand those concerns as they occur and to shoulder them with their wives.

Children long for an intimate relationship with their fathers. When that occurs, fathers will have deep, lasting respect from them and the children's mothers. Husbands, take first responsibility for the children in two areas: discipline and instruction. As Paul urged us, "Fathers, do not provoke your children to anger; but bring them up in the discipline and instruction of the Lord" (Ephesians 6:4).

Discipline

Discipline affects a child's character development. Stay involved in discipline and do not leave it primarily to your wife. Watch for power struggles between your wife and your children. Monitor your wife's emotional weariness. When it rises, check her struggle with the children. Take responsibility for special problems like tantrums or hyperactivity. Personally take care of discipline problems at school. Stay ahead by anticipating problems instead of always having to respond. Establish a relationship with each individual child and take each out alone at least once a month for an activity (or just to a restaurant) to build that relationship.

We believe spanking should be done only in the early years, and it will not be needed often if used correctly. Always explain why you are spanking, and love them tenderly afterward. As the child grows, there should be more talking and less spanking. James Dobson has written several books on the parent-child relationship that Sally and I recommend, including *Dare to Discipline* and *The Strong-Willed Child*. We also recommend *How to Really Love Your Child* and *How to Really Love Your Teenager*, both by Ross Campbell.

Instruction

Husbands, you are ultimately responsible for the spiritual development of your children. Biblical mandates are given to teach children and instruct them in the Lord, including the following key passage in Deuteronomy 6:6–7, 20–21a (NIV). (See also Psalm 78:5–8 NIV.)

> These commandments that I give you today are to be upon your hearts. Impress them on your children. Talk about them when you sit at home and when you walk along the road, when you lie down and when you get up. . . . In the future, when your son asks you, What is the meaning of the stipulations, decrees and laws the Lord our God has commanded you? 'tell him.'

Spending even an hour a week putting your children to bed is a good start. Spending personal time with them on the weekends is invaluable. Communicate with your child to find out where he or she is spiritually. Help your children solve problems. As a father, take the lead in establishing rules concerning dating and behavior with the opposite sex. Work with your wife, but keep the responsibility on your shoulders.

When possible, involve your children in establishing the rules. Make sure to set the rules before a problem develops. Anticipation is everything in child rearing. For example, don't wait until your children are fifteen to tell them they cannot date until sixteen. That's too late. Stay ahead of the game. You need to tell them at age eleven or twelve, before the need arises. They won't question the rule at that age, and will have plenty of time to tell their friends and to think about it. Establish good communication early in their lives, and it will continue, even after they leave home.

A VISION FOR YOUR MARRIAGE

"Where there is no vision, the people perish" (Proverbs 29:18 KJV). Unfortunately, most men don't have much vision for their lives. Yet, a man who seeks the Lord for life will experience fullness and joy. He and his wife will be spiritually uplifted. Consider these areas of planning for your marriage. Doing so will give direction and hope for your family.

Spiritual Responsibility

In counseling with men, I (Don) have seen tremendous need in their lives for authority and respect. I believe that for growth in Christ, men need to be dealing with spiritual issues as part of their duties. There is tremendous joy for men in church leadership, especially in a church that regards elders 'or other lay leaders' roles as a real ministry. In fact, Paul called such ministry "a fine work" (1 Timothy 3:1). If your church does not encourage personal ministry, volunteer to begin a lay program to develop spiritual responsibility. Lead a men's group, or as a couple, lead a marriage class. Become an elder or deacon if asked. God desires that you find His perspective on life, and spiritual leadership is vital to doing so. No matter what your gifts or abilities, seek counsel on a plan that helps you develop spiritual responsibilities in the home, in your church, or in Christian organizations.

Are you being mentored by someone, and are you in the process of mentoring another man? Remember the call: "The things which you have heard from me in the presence of many witnesses, entrust these to faithful men who will be able to teach others also" (2 Timothy 2:2). Remember the axiom, "We only keep what we give away."

Accountability

As much as men like to be self-confident and independent, they have deep needs for counsel from others. Such counsel may include one or more people to whom a man is accountable and consults regularly. Men have a strong need in their lives for protection from wrong decisions, for wisdom in their marriage and in child rearing, and for encouragement in their jobs.

Several times in my life, I have had to make a significant decision that was difficult for me and somewhat threatening for my family. Finding myself suddenly under considerable emotional and professional pressure, and knowing I needed to provide firm, directional family leadership, I quickly realized I could become vulnerable to Satan's inevitable attack.

To protect myself and my family, Sally and I have always had an advisory group surrounding us to give wise counsel. We usually describe our situation to them and give a historical evaluation of Sally and myself. These men and women stand with us and always give honest feedback. More importantly, they rally to our support by helping us develop an aggressive plan for the future. I usually am totally remotivated, my wife trusts and respects my openness, and I have deepened my relationship with these people. The body of Christ demands our accountability to mature believers. God says, "Without consultation, plans are frustrated, but with many counselors they succeed" (Proverbs 15:22).

The most natural place for a man to find mentors or wise counselors should be his local church. Begin to observe older couples and church leaders. Gather information concerning each leader's expertise and areas of wisdom; then cross-check your observations with the pastoral staff. After confirming your observations, decide which leader best fits your needs and seems most approachable. Ask him for a brief appointment. Most older people love to share their life experiences. If your wife and you seek joint counsel or mentoring, approach a couple. If you pray, God will lead you to the right person or couple.

In addition to looking in your church, you may find God's choice at work, in the neighborhood, or in a Bible study group. Bigger decisions many times require several counselors for better perspective and for confirmation.

Work

In Genesis 3, God instructed Adam to toil and sweat. Many men never face this fact of life. Instead, they devise all kinds of ways to get out of work like changing jobs, get-rich-quick schemes, and looking for greener grass. The times when I was unsure of my vocation were among the most frustrating and depressing periods of my life. These were also times that drove me to my knees before God.

Statistics have shown that most men change jobs several times before they discover what they really enjoy doing. About 10 percent of the male population change jobs easily, while an even larger percent tend to stay in their present job whether or not they like it. Most research indicates that the men who usually succeed in the long run are those who demonstrate perseverance in their chosen field. If you feel frustrated and inconsistent in your working experience, seek counsel. Make yourself accountable to a wiser older brother. Develop a plan to gradually refocus your job. Pursue what you enjoy and do well.

Several organizations offer helpful career assessments and feedback on finding careers where you can best use your strengths. One of them is the Life Pathways division of Christian Financial Concepts. Their "Career Direct" assessment reveals strengths in the areas of personality, skills, vocational interests, and values. For more information, call Christian Financial Concepts at 1-800-722-1976.

ELEVEN

A Woman
of Wisdom

*P*roverbs ends with verses exalting the noble wife. So honored is this woman that "her children rise up and bless her; her husband also, and he praises her, saying: 'Many daughters have done nobly, but you excel them all'" (31:28–29). Deep in her heart, every woman likes to be characterized as excellent. Hearing a husband say, "You excel them all" brings joy to any wife. If you are a wife, do you consider yourself a gift from the Lord to your husband? Would you be identified as a wise woman who is skillful at living?

"The wise woman builds her house," wrote Solomon, "but the foolish tears it down with her own hands" (Proverbs 14:1). Let's consider how wives can keep their homes and marriages strong. This chapter is for wives, to help them solidify some foundational issues and to increase in wisdom. I (Sally) hope the principles of Scripture contained here both comfort and challenge your life as a wife and daughter of God.

Over the years, Don and I have counseled and worked with many wives. We've experienced joy as their faith matured, but also cried as others missed God's perspective. Out of respect for those women and the Lord, we present the following insights.

Every woman must be able to answer four foundational questions before she can be released to enjoy life in the home:

1. Am I limited by my role as a wife?

2. What are the limits to submission?

3. Is the home my key to success as a wife?

4. How can I understand and help my husband?

If you get clear direction on these four issues, you'll have vision and wisdom in your marriage. As you read, ask God to reveal His perspective of how a woman can be fulfilled in marriage.

DOES MY ROLE AS WIFE LIMIT ME?

In the past few decades, our society has encouraged women to question and even doubt their need to have specific roles in marriage. Certainly society has challenged the scriptural calling for women. We believe, however, that the biblical role has been misunderstood: Men have seen it one way, and women the other. Considering the world's criticisms, women must have faith in God's Word and the God of the Word if they hope to maintain God's perspective. This battle must be taken seriously and approached aggressively. These truths, taken from the Word of God, are vital to experiencing God's best in marriage.

---

*W*omen are equal to men in every respect. . . .

The issue is . . . determining how God

intended most women to find expression.

Wives, God did not stack the cards against you. On the contrary, God places special significance on a woman who is a wife or mother.

As bad as society can be, without the woman' maintaining order, demonstrating love within the home, and acknowledging God's rightful place in the home, I'm not sure society would be as peaceful as it is. The issues may be tough and sometimes confusing, but God's Word remains our sure foundation.

Many women today, including Christian women, are asking, "Why must I be under a man's leadership? I deserve to be equal with a man. I am not less qualified, motivated, or capable. Yes, God, I do question your role for me."

Are women equal? Oh, yes, women are equal to men in every respect, with the single exception of physical strength. While women function differently in some ways, they too need equal expression of intellect, emotions, and physical attributes. Women should have equal opportunities publicly, as well as privately. God did not intend for women to lack expression in any way. The issue is not one of equality, but determining how God intended most women to find expression.

God's plan has never been for men and women to become more alike. God does not want the genders to become more competitive and rights oriented. Our hope lies in stepping out in faith to find fulfillment where God places us. His placement may vary with different stages of life.

I'm not talking about men and women in the workplace and marketplace. Women are not commanded to be under *any* man's leadership. She is perfectly capable to be in leadership in the workplace or in government. There are a few examples of these positions in the Bible. (Consider Deborah and Esther, for instance.) Rather, our focus, of course, is the *marriage relationship.*

In marriage, God has placed the man in the position of servant-leader, not because he is better or more qualified, but because people work better when they have structure. God knew that this was the very best structure to cause husbands and wives to function with as little discord as possible. He also knew it was the best method for raising children. In no way is God limiting either the man or the woman. Rather, He is giving them a method of fulfillment and oneness.

Women, can you trust God, knowing fully who He is? Is His plan for your life best, regardless of any momentary suffering? Admittedly, submission (or learning respect) is contrary to your human nature, and it is impossible to endure without faith. You cannot stand still in your understanding. You are either gaining or losing ground constantly.

In 1 Peter 1:12–21, Peter exhorted Christians to holiness and growth. In verse 12 he basically said, "Won't you realize that you are not serving yourselves, but God?" God's Holy Spirit gives these precious biblical promises to you. They are so great that they intrigue even angels! Remember, *submission* means to respect your husband enough to allow him leadership in your home. It is not just a trial or something you suffer. As you grow in your understanding of it through God's Word, it becomes a real blessing. You will never be more loved, appreciated, and cherished. Your needs will never be more fulfilled. You see, these are the precious promises of God Himself. Women long to be loved the way God says a husband should love.

Peter continued, "Therefore, prepare your minds for action, keep sober in spirit, fix your hope completely on the grace to be brought to you at the revelation of Jesus Christ" (verse 13). Your struggle is one of the mind. Don't allow Satan to deceive you into thinking you have a better plan than God. Decide that God can sufficiently carry you through tough situations. Often we have to put away our self-centered rights.

Peter later noted that we should not trade our hope in God for a hope in temporary or perishable things, like silver and gold (verse 18). Similarly, your hope must be placed in the proper person—the perfect Lord Jesus Christ—rather than your husband.

You will occasionally suffer in your role as a wife, but Jesus called us to follow Him, and He was perfectly submitted to His Father. Was Jesus limited in the long run by His submission? No, and neither will you be as a wife.

WHAT ARE THE LIMITS TO SUBMISSION?

The question of limits is a valid one. Scripture clearly communicates that submission by men and women alike will be tested by suffering. We can accept such suffering when it comes from doing good, but not from evil (see 2 Peter 3:17). God's Word absolutely assures the greatest blessing to the one who submits, yet no one can use submission as an excuse for sinning. God will not absolve you from responsibility for sin just because someone told you to do it and you submitted to the sinful request.

On the other hand, a wise woman will use such a request as an opportunity to be creative in understanding her husband's real need. You must ask yourself, "What is the need in my husband's life behind the request he is making?" Next, try to meet that need without contradicting Scripture.

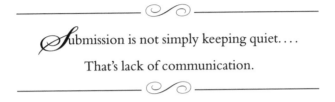

Submission is not simply keeping quiet....

That's lack of communication.

An example of submitting to the point of sin is Sapphira's response to her husband, recorded in Acts 5. Sapphira agreed to sin with Ananias, and, as a result, God took both of their lives. If your husband has asked you to do something you think is sin, seek counsel before you respond. A good advisor will give perspective and options that can honor your husband, yet not directly follow a request that violates Scripture. For most, the request will never go that far. As your husband sees your respectful attitude toward him, he will more than likely be more concerned with how you think and feel.

Another limit of submission in your role as a wife is not to submit to any physical or emotional abuse. God never intended that a husband be cruel to his wife. On the contrary, a husband is to love and serve her. If there is either physical or emotional abuse (consistently putting you down, calling you names, and so on), then counsel should be sought quickly. Many good counselors are available to deal with this devastating issue.

A word about what submission is *not* is in order. Submission is not simply keeping quiet and doing whatever your husband says. That's lack of communication. Throughout Scripture, God states that He is more interested in your heart than your actions. Let's talk about your attitudes in communication.

In an effort to help your understanding of this important area, begin by looking at the biblical command for your communication with Him: "Be anxious for nothing, but in everything by prayer and supplication with thanksgiving let your requests be made known to God. And the peace of God, which surpasses all comprehension, will guard your hearts and your minds in Christ Jesus" (Philippians 4:6–7).

God desires for you to express to Him not only your needs, but your very wants. He doesn't promise to give you your wants, although many times in His grace, He does. He does promise peace beyond your understanding. The key thought is that He wants you to tell Him your wants, to talk to Him. What is prayer but simply talking to God? Now if God wants you to talk with Him, would He ask that wives not talk to their husbands? Absolutely not! That would be a contradiction of Scripture.

Your hope should never be in your husband's ability . . . to change, but in the Lord, who does the changing.

What God is saying in this passage is, "Women, if your husband has an attitude of being disobedient to God's Word, then do not provoke him further by nagging or hitting him with Bible verses again and again." Instead, inwardly make a faith decision to trust God at that moment, so you can outwardly win your husband with your positive actions. You must place your hope in God, not your husband, and allow him to be wrong—even fail—so that the Lord can convict him. You simply love and encourage him by how you treat him. "Let your speech always be with grace, as though seasoned with salt, so that you will know how you should respond to each person" (Colossians 4:6).

Once you have told your husband you think he is wrong in some way, don't continue to harp on that issue. Turn it over to God and let Him deal with it. A wife should be able to express her opinions freely and lovingly; in fact, her husband will want her to do so.

However, your hope should never be in your husband's ability or willingness to change, but in the Lord, who does the changing. You want him to know how you feel about the matter. But you must assure him that you love him, no matter what, and that you will support him in prayer. Then wait for God to work in his life.

The balance to this freedom to communicate feelings is the strong warning God gives about the poison of our mouths. In Romans 3, Paul wrote that the mouth is "an open grave" (verse 13) capable of unbelievable destruction. James taught that we should be slow to anger and slow to speak, or we will lose God's blessing (James 1:19–20). A good thermometer of a respectful wife is how she uses her mouth. Proverbs 15 declares, "A gentle answer turns away wrath. . . . How delightful is a timely word!" (verses 1, 23).

If a woman has God's perspective, she will do the following:

1. Wait for the proper time to tell her husband her negative thoughts.

2. Talk to the Lord about it in the meantime.

3. Speak peaceably when the time comes—without anger, bitterness, resentment, or belittling.

4. Trust the Lord for the outcome even when no change is seen.

When it comes to communication, remember that men and women are different. We never come at the same problem the same way. Both perspectives are needed to solve problems.

IS THE HOME THE KEY TO MY SUCCESS AS A WIFE?

With all the negative publicity homemakers have been getting in recent years, along with the glamour attributed to the working woman, it's no surprise that wives question their vocation in the home. I constantly run into young wives who plan to have children at a late age or don't intend to have children at all. They say they cannot fully express themselves in the home. More and more wives are attributing their struggles in life to being captive to the house and the children. Again, the question must be asked, "Did God make a mistake by placing wives and mothers in the home?"

Because of the importance and diligence necessary in a home-maker's responsibilities, we must emphasize the value of the home. Close on the heels of Satan's deceit concerning submission is his deceit concerning the value of the home. With the help of our culture, Satan has convinced women that their existence in the home is a barrier to fulfillment. Once a woman's eyes focus on herself instead of God, she begins a lonely uphill battle. The many struggles of the home quickly wear her down and defeat her spirit of hope, resulting in fear—the enemy of faith.

While it is OK for women to have careers,

it is best for mothers to stay at home

with children once they arrive.

Note the consistent pattern of Satan. He first catches a woman in a struggle (and a homemaker has plenty of them). At that point of conflict, the woman's consciousness of God's presence is low. Being deceived, she does not directly doubt God; instead, she places the blame on her husband or the home situation. The moment a woman sees a person or responsibility in the home as the problem, her commitment is broken. She then begins to subconsciously resent and rebel against the one she blames: her husband (but ultimately the Lord). Once she has begun to resent or rebel, her whole relationship with God and her family is affected.

Yes, the home *is* the key to a wife's success. While it is OK for women to have careers, it is best for mothers to stay at home with children once they arrive. Children are given to us by God to raise and nurture for only eighteen years. This is a very short but important time in our lives and theirs. During the formative years, it is vital that Mom remains in the home for many reasons: security, faith training, time spent with children, early education, love, and physical attention. There usually are some creative alternatives to working full time: working three days a week, getting home by three o'clock, computer work in the home, and so on.

Years ago the feminist movement rose to power by exhibiting proof of the plight of the average woman. I agree with the movement on issues of equal pay for equal work, but I disagree on two major issues: the cause of the homemaker's problems and the solutions offered. In essence, these women were saying that it is a mistake to have defined roles, either in or out of the home. While our country has rightly tried to give freedom of expression to women in the workplace, leaders have done a poor job of communicating the importance of being a wife and a mother. I am not downplaying the fact that many women work outside the home, some because of desire, others because of economic necessity, and still others without children at home. But far too often women mistakenly believe they cannot be fulfilled without working outside the home. Nothing could be farther from the truth.

Putting work outside the home on hold . . .

will require an adjustment in the family finances,

since there will only be one paycheck.

Many women make the mistake of thinking that they are no longer needed in the home when the child enters school and therefore reenter the workplace. Children still need Mom at home at *every* age. It is particularly important for mothers to stay at home during the teen years. Many temptations occur naturally for teens when Mom is not at home: sex, crime, pornography, and drugs. Add to this the fact that most other moms in the neighborhood work. Therefore, you may be one of the few moms to whom kids will come and talk after school. This certainly was true for all four of our children in their teen years. I was there to answer questions for them and for their friends. We opened our home for ministries such as Young Life and Fellowship of Christian Athletes, and kids were welcome in our home, day or night. The challenge as parents is to influence your children and their friends with religious and moral values.

This may mean putting work outside the home on hold. In *Women Leaving the Workplace,* author Larry Burkett points out that this will require an adjustment in the family finances, since there will only be one paycheck. The benefit will be having more time to make the home a genuine haven for the family. When your children leave home for college, you'll then be free to pursue a career, more education, a ministry to other women, or even to travel with your husband. You'll feel good about the time you spent with your children, and will not wish you could do it over.

The wise, woman will search for God's perspective and His personal will for her life, using Scripture as the primary standard. This in no way limits her in the home or in the workplace. It is a matter of God's calling and timing in her life.

A GODLY PERSPECTIVE

Proverbs 31 describes a godly woman who is creative in and out of her home. Since no woman could ever accomplish all that she did, I believe this example is written for women of all eras to show the unlimited possibilities of a godly woman. Her mind held different values than we see the world teaching us today. Her mental freedom allowed her creativity to flow.

Listen to God's description of this woman's life, mentioned in the final two verses of Proverbs: "Charm is deceitful and beauty is vain, but a woman who fears the Lord, she shall be praised. Give her the product of her hands, and let her works praise her in the gates" (Proverbs 31:30–31).

The word *charm* describes a superficial graciousness, and the word used for *beauty* means "vaporous." God is saying that the woman who places her hope in her superficiality or temporary youthful attractiveness is headed for disaster. But the woman who fears the Lord shall find total expression and praise. The term *fear* means "reverential awe," meaning she doesn't question God's plan for her as a woman. She doesn't place her hope in the ideologies of the world, but instead commits her hope to the Lord and His view of life.

This woman is promised—and receives—praise. The product of her hands is her home and all that it contains. The gates are the public places. She is known by what her home (her husband and each child) turns out to be. God may call some women out of the home, but I believe that the home is the greatest place for most wives to find fulfillment. When people are asked about their mothers, they usually don't talk about what she does. Rather, most focus on her character—who she is.

Significantly, this godly woman is characterized by hope and by work: "Strength and dignity are her clothing, and she smiles at the future. She opens her mouth in wisdom, and the teaching of kindness is on her tongue. She looks well to the ways of her household, and does not eat the bread of idleness" (verses 25–27).

Here is a woman of stature! She is not defeated by a woe-is-me attitude. *Strength* and *dignity* indicate she is a confident woman whose compassion and love free her of future worry. Her faith brings her success, and hope fills her heart.

This woman is able to smile at the future. She does not fear it because she has prepared her household for it physically, emotionally, and spiritually. As she meets the needs of her husband and children, her needs are met. She teaches wisdom and skill in the art of living by teaching biblical truths to her children so that they too will follow the Lord. She leads them to salvation and instructs them in their walk with Him. In order to do this, she spends personal time with the Lord and views her work positively. Her role is so fulfilling and far-reaching that she thanks the Lord for the privilege of being a wife and mother.

The Proverbs 31 woman is emotionally and physically able to work hard and sacrificially, "and does not eat the bread of idleness." Idleness is destructive to a woman's self-image and her spiritual walk. Since the godly woman doesn't resent being needed, she is available to meet the needs of her household.

Note also (in verses 13–24) that this woman has a great diversity in her work that takes her in and out of the home. Women who suffer anxiety over their role in the home typically lack diversity in daily tasks, not overwork. Women need both tasks that involve people and stimulate their intellect, as well as give them authority. Work is vital to life. It takes hard work to raise children properly and to run a household well—tasks that are neither mindless nor trivial.

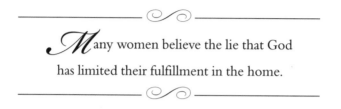

Many women believe the lie that God has limited their fulfillment in the home.

Finally, the godly wife is creative with her abilities and displays much energy. Among the many duties (see verses 13–16), she looks for clothing material (wool and flax), shops in far places, cooks, buys and sells property, tends to a garden (vineyard), and sews. She also works in community affairs with the poor and needy (verse 20), makes and sells clothes (verse 24), and teaches in the community (verse 26).

Any way you look at her, she is not limited privately or publicly. Few men have the freedom to be as far-reaching and diversified as this woman, and yet many women believe the lie that God has limited their fulfillment in the home. The truth is, men are motivated by these types of women and their positive attitudes toward the home. The Proverbs 31 woman is wise enough to believe God, and her family praises her for her steadfastness.

Many women say they want opportunities to do more things. If you plan to be active, you will need physical stamina. It is no little thing that God states, "She girds herself with strength and makes her arms strong" (verse 17). A godly woman seeks to maintain her energy level and usually succeeds.

In counseling, I am amazed at the number of women who are physically tired. If a woman says she is tired, it is hard to ask her to do more. Many women believe the way to restore lost energy is to rest more. That may be true in momentary cases of exhaustion, but with any long-term problem, the opposite is often true. Exercise will actually increase your energy level. Our friend in Proverbs 31 kept herself strong and her energy level high. If you are overly exhausted, see a doctor. Otherwise, staying active is good for both your physical and mental health.

The result of this wife's efforts is the praise of her husband and children. God structured the emotions of children and the desires of husbands to naturally seek her. Because self-worth and self-expression can only be measured by relating to people and to God, this was a gracious act of God. In our case, five people naturally run to me: Don and my four kids! Have you ever noticed that when big football players say "Hi" on TV, they usually say "Hi, Mom!" Very few say, "Hi, Dad!" or anyone else! Mothers are so loved and revered.

What a fantastic honor to be a wife and mother!

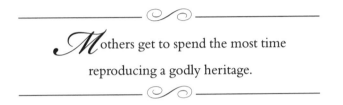

Mothers get to spend the most time reproducing a godly heritage.

As mothers, we receive the awesome God-given privilege of bearing and raising children. Mothers get to spend the most time reproducing a godly heritage. A mother uniquely understands each child and his or her emotional makeup. She gets to answer the majority of their questions. She gets to guide them into most of the spiritual truth they learn. It's her heart they hear the most. As children grow, they run to Mom when hurt or when trouble confronts them. Often she is the first to hear about whom they love and want to marry. She gets to help plan their weddings. It is her skirts that cradle the new grandchildren. I can't think of a better and more rewarding job!

Since this role has critical generational effects, don't sell your children and grandchildren short by not spending time with them. Together with your husband, practice the biblical mandates given to parents to teach and instruct children in the Lord. (See in particular Deuteronomy 6:6–7, 20; Psalm 78:5–8.)

So what are the keys to success for a married woman?

- Constantly seek God's perspective on life.

- Become a model by serving your husband and children.

- Allow God to meet your needs through your husband, children, and opportunities in your home.

- Remember that outside activities, including a career, can be fulfilling if the needs in your home have been met first.

- Find a woman's group or Bible study to help encourage your own spiritual growth. Your own spiritual health is vitally important to nurturing the family God has given you.

HOW CAN I UNDERSTAND AND HELP MY HUSBAND?

A quick review of trends impacting American men will illustrate how women can be supportive of their husbands.

As women of this generation shout, "I am not going to take this oppression anymore," men are suffering unbearably themselves. The pressures on the job and in society affect men's health, including their mortality. After age twenty-four, 20 percent more men commit suicide than women. After age forty, men die at a quicker rate than women.[1]

What is happening to American men? It is not a simple question. Since the culture seems to strike hardest at the role of men, try to understand some of their struggles.

Men are frustrated because they no longer experience natural authority over those in their care.

Few men own a home without debt, and less own land. Almost all men work for someone else. With loan institutions or bosses in firm control, men typically feel helpless or fear a lack of dominion over their lives. Furthermore, men are frustrated because they no longer experience natural authority over those in their care. The authoritarian influence of the past has turned into the democratic home of the twentieth century. The father is often just another vote in the family. No wonder the lack of male leadership is one of the greatest problems in America, even among Christian men. Husbands experience anxiety and loss of personal dignity in their families, leading to a role identity crisis for many. In turn, this crisis tends to promote hostility toward or withdrawal from their wives.

Today, there is a lack of effective male role models for young men. With more than one-third of American children coming from broken homes, young men move through their developmental years without observing assertive, confident, and sensitive men of direction. Many young men have no concept of what a father is, does, and should be. Girls also lack the fatherly love so necessary to a healthy maturing process and, as a result, often have more difficulty in the sexual area because they crave male attention.

Help by Avoiding Comparison

To answer the question, "How can a wife help her husband?" begin by realizing that just as women must confront the superwoman image, men are affected deeply by the tremendous pressure of comparison with other fantasy supermen images. The mass media offer daily the powerful president, the wise senator, the handsome executive, or the stylish athlete. Husbands receive little incentive to develop a man's inner qualities, such as faithfulness and consistency. Instead, more emphasis is placed on outer qualities, such as athletic ability, wealth, and appearance. A man can, over time, become discouraged with the barrage of comparison and competition.

The godly woman must be realistic about who her husband is and also be able to envision what he can become. Without a plan or direction from God, the natural tendency would be to ignore these things. But a woman who desires to be a godly wife to her husband will look beyond his weaknesses, encouraging him toward total fulfillment.

Women, your highest calling as wives is to understand, love, and help your husbands to be fulfilled, motivated, and responsible men. Do not compare your husband to other men and find him wanting. Instead, envision his potential even as God does, and encourage him to pursue it.

Help by Showing Compassion

In the same way, a wife should not allow her dissatisfaction with her husband to overshadow her compassion for him. Compassion is a deep, unselfish concern for another. God knows that our husbands will discourage us at times as well, yet He desires that we experience the best. Therefore, as Christ does, we should show compassion for our husbands.

It's not uncommon for a wife to lose perspective concerning her husband's weaknesses. In fact, she can become so discouraged and distrustful of her mate that she can no longer believe God will work through him. The husband's failure causes her to nag. Proverbs speaks of such a woman: "A constant dripping on a day of steady rain and a contentious woman are alike; he who would restrain her restrains the wind, and grasps oil with his right hand" (Proverbs 27:15–16).

A wife who constantly nags her husband in a quarrelsome and strife-ridden way will soon be unwilling to follow his leadership. Reversing that process will be more difficult than stopping the wind or grasping oil in your hand, according to God's Word.

Often a wife will ask Don if he would lead her husband to Christ or convince him of some spiritual truth. She usually has made matters worse by asking several women's groups to pray for him. Instead, she needs to start by realizing that her attitude of spiritual superiority toward him has usually angered or discouraged him over a period of time. This man is really rejecting his wife's attitude, not Christ. If we can get her to ask her husband's forgiveness and love him for who he is, the husband is usually open to talking about a God powerful enough to get his wife to say she was wrong!

Wives also say, "If you could just get my husband to spend more time with the children, things would be fine." Unfortunately, a wife may have so covered their husbands with guilt and rejection that every time the children enter the room, the father subconsciously feels whipped. These feelings retard a man's natural aggressiveness, and make him want to shun his own children because they are a reminder of his failures. Hardly anyone is motivated like this. By trusting her children to God first, a wife can then ask a husband's forgiveness for judging him, and give him the freedom to spend time with the kids as he feels he should. This man is free to be convicted by the Lord without being sidetracked by feelings of anger and rejection.

I have seen men treat new cars better than their wives. Why? Because a car is their total, unabridged responsibility. God created men to sense and respond to real dependence. They naturally feel more responsible for a wife who's there for better or worse.

An attentive wife knows how to please her husband. Your husband has tremendous demands placed upon his life from all directions. Often you cannot control those outside demands, but you can control your attitudes of love and acceptance toward your husband. You can cause him to look forward to coming home.

Help Him by Knowing His Needs

Scripture teaches that your husband has certain God-given needs that must be fulfilled: needs to protect, to own, to have authority, to be productive, to love, and to reproduce his image. Let's look at eight of these needs. (Some are mentioned briefly, since they are covered in more detail elsewhere.) Consider the areas where you can specifically help him meet his needs.

First, every husband has a need to trust. There are fragile areas of every spouse's life that he/she does not want or need the public to know. These intimacies should be shared just between the two of you and aren't meant for anyone else. He needs to confide in someone he can trust, and a wife has an opportunity to fulfill that role. Don't breach his trust in you. Of the noble wife it's said, "The heart of her husband trusts in her, and he will have no lack of gain. She does him good and not evil all the days of her life" (Proverbs 31:11–12).

Second, every husband has vocational needs. Usually a man's work sets the pattern for the other areas of his life. A man satisfied with his work is a happy man. A wife is in an excellent position to study her husband to see what he enjoys doing. Watch him play as well as work, since many times what he does with his free time reveals what he really enjoys. Encourage and uplift your mate in his work. Many men enjoy what they are doing, but secretly feel others do not adequately respect them for it. Hearing that you are proud of him can make a tremendous difference to your husband since he deeply desires your respect.

Be willing to adjust your spending and standard of living to allow your husband to change his career, if necessary. Even if the change brings the family a lower salary and a lower living standard, be willing to accept the adjustments of a potential move or different work hours—after, of course, discussion and recognizing this is the leading of the Lord. Anything you do to stabilize and increase his happiness helps you, too. A man has an almost constant need in life to reevaluate his vocation. He needs the freedom of knowing his wife will support him in all his endeavors.

Third, every husband has spiritual needs. Scripture places significant importance on spiritual leadership in a man's life. Encourage any inclination your husband shows toward taking spiritual responsibility. Especially after age thirty, a man's feeling of importance can be increased if he is involved in church leadership or in a discipleship process. This may require you to have a Bible study in your home or to make friends with the spouses of your husband's friends. Whatever it takes, help all you can. If your husband is not gifted in public ministry, perhaps he can facilitate small groups in your church—an excellent way to develop his leadership skills.

He needs a refuge in his home,

away from the business of his workday.

However, don't push him. Pressuring him to lead a group won't be beneficial if his spiritual gifts lie in other areas such as service or helps. Remember, God does the motivating. Always encourage your husband in his spiritual leadership, reminding him of opportunities in the home. This includes leading in thankgiving at mealtime, directing family devotions, and praying with and for you and the family. A husband does not need to be outgoing to lead his family spiritually and to develop his own spiritual life.

Fourth, every husband has sexual needs. This need is very important to most men, and detailed information is contained in chapter 13. Recognizing the differing sexual needs between men and women is very helpful in understanding that your husband is very normal.

Fifth, every husband has a need for time alone. Recognize that often your husband may think and solve problems in his mind before he talks about them. The opposite is not true of women. Sometimes he brings issues from the workday home with him. He needs a refuge in his home, away from the business of his workday. Men usually bury themselves in the newspaper, TV, the home office, or bedroom to unwind. A wise wife gives him some down time before engaging in conversation or having him play with the children.

Sixth, every husband has relationship needs. Many husbands are loners. If you add to those the large number of couples who do not develop mutual friends, the problem becomes staggering. Relationships are very important in a man's life. You receive benefits from your husband's relationships, including better communication, diversity of interests, and increased hope in life. Observe people your husband naturally likes and create social settings where he feels comfortable. When possible, pursue his interests with friends. The more you do sacrificially for him, the more he will return the blessing.

Seventh, every husband has intellectual needs. Do what you can to recognize your husband's intellectual interests. Initiate a mutual discussion on an issue, and your husband will look forward to sharing his thoughts with you. A husband who feels his wife cares about his intellectual interests feels a special closeness with her. She becomes a real friend. In addition, if she listens to him in even one area, he can then listen to her in other areas without feeling she is preaching.

Eighth, every husband has authoritative needs. A wife who encourages her husband's leadership in her life is a protected woman. This sounds good, but how do you do it? Two ways to give your husband authority and revive his natural desire to protect you are to praise him and place your hope in God alone.

A wife who encourages her husband's

leadership in her life is a protected woman.

The mother is a model to the children. If she doesn't respect him, neither will they. Give your children a blessing by insisting that they respect their father. Praise their dad to them for what he has done. Children can also have a powerful influence on the dad. If the wife is complimentary when not in his presence, the children will compliment him to his face.

Verbal praise is extremely vital to a man. When a wife praises her husband, it demonstrates her love for him. When she is critical, it shows she does not understand the faith perspective of marriage. "An anxious heart weighs a man down, but a kind word cheers him up" (Proverbs 12:25 NIV).

Remember, God gave the mandate for wives to submit, or respect, their husbands. Why? Because respect is the greatest need for men.

A wise woman releases her husband to take leadership in her life by placing her hope in God. She allows him to be fully mature—including letting him make mistakes without recriminations—because she views him as a gift from God with no limitation to her fulfillment. The Holy Spirit is then free to help her understand her husband in particular and the differences in men and women in general.

Let's become women whose "pleasant words are a honeycomb, sweet to the soul and healing to the bones" (Proverbs 16:24).

NOTE

1. *World Almanac and Book of Facts* (Mahwah, N.J.: Funk and Wagnalls, 1996).

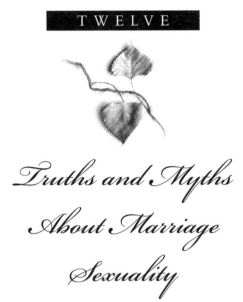

TWELVE

Truths and Myths About Marriage Sexuality

Sex. What a powerful drive God created in men and women! Anyone considering marriage, and those already married, should plan to fully pursue sexual expression within marriage. You might say, "What an unnecessary statement! Sure, I plan to do just that." Yet marriage counselors all over America report that couples mention the sexual relationship as one of their most difficult areas of struggle.

God has much to say about sexuality in Scripture, leaving no doubt about its importance to marital love. He also created sexual love to require faith. It should be no surprise that God wants you to depend on Him in this area. Once again, knowing Scripture will allow the Holy Spirit to both teach and convict you. Open your mind and heart to the Holy Spirit as you read God's directions.

This chapter will look at the myths of sexual expression and the biblical truths and guidelines that free husbands and wives to express their sexuality in healthy, loving ways. Our discussion of sexual expression in marriage is so important that we will conclude it in chapter 13 with a look at three key topics: (1) sexual differences between men and women, (2) advice to men and women, and (3) dealing with past or recent premarital sexual encounters.

Before we look at problems and myths in the sexual relationship, a word of encouragement. First and foremost for a successful sexual relationship, *remember that God created sexual expression. He fully intended pleasure and blessing in its creation.* Israel's King Solomon and his young wife from Shulim stated it best:

"How beautiful you are, my darling, how beautiful you are! Your eyes are like doves."

"How handsome you are, my beloved, and so pleasant! Indeed, our couch is luxuriant!'" (Song of Solomon 1:15–16)

This is only one of many biblical passages that express the excitement and happiness God intended for marital love. Discerning God's intention for the physical relationship to be a blessing will go a long way toward mental and physical enjoyment of one another.

WHY PROBLEMS DEVELOP

Though God has intended blessing for marriages, many Christian couples develop problems in the marriage bed.

"I am angry and bitterly disappointed about my sexual experience," a Christian woman once told us. "I was so expectant and excited when I got married, only to find shock and mediocrity," she said. "It is not at all what I had thought it would be. What surprises me most is that I am probably more of a problem than my husband."

We never cease to be amazed at the number of men and women who say similar things three or four years into marriage. It is not necessary for this to happen.

There are three basic reasons why couples experience frustration in this most intimate of relationships. The primary cause of frustration is the cultural programming they have received. The film and television industries create false sexual images. The media subtly imply that only physically attractive people really succeed sexually and that great sexual compatability comes quickly and easily. Movies seldom depict sexual failure or growth! Reality is ignored and replaced with a fantasy image, which somehow escapes us in the reality of the bedroom. Meanwhile, the wholesale merchandising of sex by advertisers has contributed significantly to the growth of pornography. False comparison, false images, guilt, and disappointment reign in our culture as a result. These factors confuse us, leaving us unsure of what God really desires for us sexually.

The second major cause of sexual frustration today is the nature of human beings. As we have mentioned numerous times, men and women are self-centered beings.

Problems in the sexual relationship are a prime example. Self-centeredness in any area can devastate a marriage, but that is particularly true with sex and romance. Each partner brings to the bedroom different standards, desires, and inhibitions about sex. Each may carry a certain amount of scar tissue from the past. Pride is also involved. We want to be self-sufficient and, therefore, we don't want to admit we don't know it all. We have difficulty asking for help. We tend to blame our spouses when sex isn't as exciting as we dreamed it would be, or as Hollywood portrays it to be.

The third major cause of sexual problems results from the lack of quality Christian teaching on sex. For the most part, Christian leadership has not responded well to people's needs in this area, and has not taught positive truths from God's Word concerning sex. When there were attempts in the past, the teaching was often legalistic: a bunch of no's, without answers to "why not?" questions.

Most couples we have worked with in counseling and seminars tell us they never have received specific instructions on sex from anyone with authority in their lives. Our culture, man's nature, and ineffective teaching have resulted in a sexually frustrated society.

CULTURAL AND RELIGIOUS
MYTHS CONCERNING SEX

Over the centuries, human nature and the poor cultural models have produced sexual hang-ups in couples. Before couples can escape this entrapment, those patterns must be identified. Usually identifying them will help couples begin the process of overriding their effects. Occasionally, it may be necessary to seek help from a professional Christian counselor.

———————— ❧ ————————

The virile male typically is portrayed as a "Ready Freddie"—always ready to perform sexually.

———————— ❧ ————————

We have indicated that the film and television industries have contributed to sexual struggles in marriage by creating false sexual images. This certainly is true in the image of the so-called "all-American" male. The virile male typically is portrayed as a "Ready Freddie"—always ready to perform sexually. The man who is not instantaneously ready at all times may be suspected of being less of a man. Men and women alike subject themselves to this thinking. The result is that men may try to prove themselves on the one hand, or they may develop insecurity about their manhood, thinking they should be more aggressive and successful. Either of these can add real pressure to their sexual experience. Women who accept this image are often surprised and sometimes frustrated that their husband does not act like the infamous "Ready Freddie."

All things considered, a man's sexual motivation and function are not all that different from a woman's. He experiences times of low interest also, and may need sensitivity and motivation from his wife. Generally speaking, however, men think about sex more often than women at any given age. This is not abnormal, wives!

And what about the women's expectations? Unlike the men, most women who remain virgins before marriage need an adjustment period before becoming an aggressive lover after marriage. It is important to note that if a woman has a healthy relationship with her father and a healthy relationship with the Lord, she will have fewer problems adjusting to her sexual relationship.

Early experimentation with sex or having multiple sex partners before marriage may produce guilt and/or problems with desire on the part of the female. The same experiences by the male may make the man overly aggressive sexually toward his wife. Wise counsel may be needed to overcome past experiences. (This will be discussed more in the final section of the next chapter.)

As your wife seeks God's perspective, you should exhibit tremendous sensitivity, patience, and acceptance. Your goal should be to motivate her sexually by loving her unconditionally.

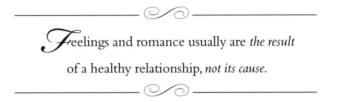

Feelings and romance usually are *the result*

of a healthy relationship, *not its cause.*

The other prevalent myth about sexual expression concerns romance and sexual desire. Couples must realize that the media helped to create false images concerning sexual desire. These false images communicate, "If you really love me, you will naturally want to have sex." Certainly any agape marriage will experience romance and sexual desire, but feelings and romance usually are *the result* of a healthy relationship, *not its cause.* Throughout the marriage, a couple should dialogue often to discover new ways to sexual and romantic excitement.

Romance is not automatic. Time, effort, and creativity must be invested in the relationship before romance blossoms. Understanding God's Word, seeking counsel, and having open communication will cause the sexual union to succeed over time.

BIBLICAL TRUTHS ABOUT THE SEXUAL RELATIONSHIP

In Scripture, God has spoken boldly concerning sexual matters. To understand His perspective, begin by learning the Biblical absolutes concerning sexual love. The following ten truths are of vital importance to a successful and healthy sexual relationship because they represent the guideposts for spiritual counsel on sexual matters.

Truth 1: Sexuality is God's Creation

It is important that every man and woman realize that God unquestionably created his or her sexuality. Genesis 1:27 says, "God created man in His own image, in the image of God He created him; male and female He created them." Physical anatomies represent one of the most significant differences in God's creation of male and female. These differences affect all our being, from our moods and emotions to our perspectives.

Clearly, God created man and woman as different sexual entities with the opportunity to become "one flesh." The creation of sexual differences was no accident, but a deliberate part of God's unique plan. God designed you to accept your sexuality and to seek positive fulfillment in marriage. Hollywood did not create sex—God did! And since everything that He created was very good (Genesis 1:31), you are free to seek its fullness. Sex can be fun, creative, and very rewarding. Solomon and his Shulammite wife knew this.

Truth 2: Physical Love Is for Procreation *and* Pleasure

The second major reality from Scripture is that God intended sex and marriage to produce children *and* for pleasure. Sometimes we remember the first reason but ignore the second. But both are divine purposes of physical oneness.

There are exceptions, but the emphasis is clear. God created both sex and children to be a blessing. Therefore, sex and marriage give you a wonderful picture of God's love for you. The love you experience for your children gives you a small glimpse as to how much love God has for you.

---

*W*ithout a doubt, God associates pleasure

and excitement with the sexual relationship.

Children give couples the opportunity to reproduce not only God's image, but their images as well (see, for example, Genesis 5:3). God created sex for procreation. He had commanded Adam and Eve to be fruitful and multiply and fill the earth (Genesis 1:28), and Solomon wrote, "Behold, children are a gift of the Lord; the fruit of the womb is a reward (Psalm 127:3).

The world promotes the concept that sex is a natural instinct. But God designed sex to be the result of total expression between a husband and wife. Sex was never meant to be shared apart from the unity of the marriage relationship. Children were to be a result of the unique and permanent relationship between the husband and wife.

Significantly, God refers to sexual relations in the opening chapters of Genesis in the context of *blessing*—a word that refers to a high state of joy and pleasure. God devotes a whole book of the Bible to describing this blessing and its associated joys: Song of Solomon. Here the Bible has said of sexual love, "Its flashes are flashes of fire, the very flame of the Lord" (8:6). Without a doubt, God associates pleasure and excitement with the sexual relationship. Solomon used romantic, sensuous language when he declared a wife to be "a loving doe, a graceful deer," and urged the husband, "May her breasts satisfy you always, may you ever be captivated by her love" (Proverbs 5:19 NIV).

Truth 3: Physical Love Demands a Time Priority

In 1 Corinthians 7 and in the Song of Solomon, God implies that successful lovemaking requires a time priority. Solomon created a special bedroom and took his bride away from the activities of life. The preparation and time taken imply that God ordained special emphasis in sexual matters. Is your bedroom a special place?

In Deuteronomy 24:5, young men were instructed: "When a man takes a new wife, he shall not go out with the army nor be charged with any duty; he shall be free at home one year and shall give happiness to his wife whom he has taken." The words "give happiness" refer to sexual pleasure. Since older men of God knew how vital the sexual relationship was to marriage, they placed sex above other very important matters to allow the couple to initially establish their sexual relationship. Any couple who expects to be sexually satisfied must spend time developing their relationship. Not only is the honeymoon important; the years that follow require time and effort to maintain mutual satisfaction.

Truth 4: Physical Love Requires a Transfer of Body Ownership

Sexual love is so important to Christian marriage that the Scripture suggests that couples exchange rights to their own bodies for the sake of their sexual oneness. "The husband must fulfill his duty to his wife, and likewise also the wife to her husband. The wife does not have authority over her own body, but the husband does; and likewise also the husband does not have authority over his own body, but the wife does" (1 Corinthians 7:3–4).

This command clearly establishes God's commitment to physical oneness in marriage. Gracious sacrifice is part of every sexual union from God's perspective. Your body is not yours, but your mate's. God wants you to trust Him and give your body for your mate's pleasure. God intends this to be for mutual pleasure and not for selfish purposes. God makes sex a sacrificial act that is redemptive in that it gets your eyes off your needs and onto the needs of your mate.

Truth 5: Physical Love Is Passionate and Creative

The Song of Solomon describes Solomon and his wife expressing their sexual union in creative and passionate terms. Through this divinely inspired "Song of Songs" (1:1), God implies that mutual sexual communication is needed. Both the wife and the husband must creatively communicate their sexual thoughts and desires. In several passages, Solomon excitedly describes his wife's body. The Shulammite bride responds with an equally passionate description of Solomon's body (4:1–7; 5:10–16; 7:1–9). Study the two passages and feel free to smile at the language used.

> "How beautiful are your feet in sandals, O prince's daughter! The curves of your hips are like jewels, the work of the hands of an artist. Your navel is like a round goblet which never lacks mixed wine; your belly is like a heap of wheat fenced about with lilies. Your two breasts are like two fawns, twins of a gazelle. Your neck is like a tower of ivory, your eyes like the pools in Heshbon by the gate of Bath-rabbim; your nose is like the tower of Lebanon, which faces toward Damascus. Your head crowns you like Carmel, and the flowing locks of your head are like purple threads; the king is captivated by your tresses." (Song of Solomon 7:1–5)

Notice that Solomon's eyes start at her feet, progress to the midsection, on to her head, then back to the midsection (verses 6–8). His primary interest is her midsection. He is physical.

In contrast, the wife's interest is different:

> "My beloved is dazzling and ruddy, outstanding among ten thousand. His head is like gold, pure gold; his locks are like clusters of dates and black as a raven. His eyes are like doves beside streams of water, bathed in milk, and reposed in their setting. His cheeks are like a bed of balsam, banks of sweet-scented herbs; his lips are lilies, dripping with liquid myrrh. His hands are rods of gold set with beryl; his abdomen is carved ivory inlaid with sapphires. His legs are pillars of alabaster set on pedestals of pure gold; his appearance is like Lebanon, choice as the cedars. His mouth is full of sweetness. And he is wholly desirable. This is my beloved and this is my friend, O daughters of Jerusalem." (Song of Solomon 5:10–16)

She starts with his head, proceeds to his abdomen, legs, and then back to his head. Clearly, the Shulammite is primarily interested in Solomon's face. She is relational. His face reflects his person—the compelling aspect of her relationship with him.

In 6:13, Solomon describes a dance the Shulammite does to excite him sexually. Mutual pleasure can be explored this way with God's blessing. Creative and passionate marital love is good in the sight of God. Hebrews 13:4 says, "Marriage is to be held in honor among all, and the marriage bed is to be undefiled."

Truth 6: Scripture Advocates Sexual Verbalization

In Song of Solomon 2:6, the Shulammite gives specific instructions during the act of making love: "Let his left hand be under my head and his right hand embrace me." In 4:16, she adds, "Awake . . . make my garden breathe out fragrance . . . May my beloved come into his garden and eat its choice fruits!"

God demonstrates how significant verbalizing one's desires is to sexual love. Yet sexual communication is difficult for most people when first married. Learning to verbalize in marriage becomes more comfortable as time passes. Expressing your thoughts and feelings concerning sexuality pays great dividends as you mature together. Avoid being negative during the sexual act. Instead, it's helpful to communicate briefly sexual preferences. The day after your sexual encounter, inquire what you can do to improve your partner's satisfaction. (We will revisit this truth in chapter 13 under "Sexual Verbalization.")

Truth 7: Physical Love Should Occur Regularly

God specifically instructs married couples to have sexual relations regularly. He warns that disobeying this command leaves the partners open to a loss of self-control, that is, lust problems, which could include sexual fantasies about other women, pornographic materials, masturbation, or even affairs. "Stop depriving one another, except by agreement for a time, so that you may devote yourselves to prayer, and come together again so that Satan will not tempt you because of your lack of self-control," Paul warned (1 Corinthians 7:5).

The issue here is not to establish a standard for the number of times to have intercourse per week. Instead, the focus is to have regular, mutually satisfying sexual contact. Notice that there is no age limit mentioned. The Bible gives accounts of sexual love for the elderly. Abraham and Sarah enjoyed sexual relations in their nineties as Sarah conceived and gave birth to Isaac (Genesis 21:2–6). Regularity may change, but there are biblical, medical, and psychological reasons why the sexual relationship is as important at age sixty as it is at age twenty-five.

Song of Solomon 5:1 says "Eat, O friends, and drink; drink your fill, O lovers" (NIV). Your fill may be different from that of other couples. God wants you as a couple to determine what is mutually satisfying in your unique relationship, both in regularity and in creativity.

Truth 8: Physical Love Is More Than Physical

Don't focus on the physical aspects of sexuality to the neglect of the emotional, spiritual, and intellectual needs. Scripture never makes this mistake. When God said Adam and Eve were naked and unashamed, He was plainly speaking of more than physical transparency. When studying the Song of Solomon, notice that this couple's communication incorporates one another's total needs. The Shulammite rejects Solomon momentarily (5:2–8). He responds to her with love and blessing (6:4–10). The importance of the total person in lovemaking is evident. God compares the union of husband and wife with the union of Christ and His church (Ephesians 5:32).

I highly recommend chapters 2 and 3 of Tim LaHaye's book, *The Act of Marriage,* because they communicate the wholeness of the individual man and woman.

Truth 9: Physical Love Gives Comfort and Healing

David and Bathsheba were utterly distraught following the death of their baby. "Then David comforted his wife Bathsheba, and he went to her and lay with her. She gave birth to a son, and they named him Solomon" (2 Samuel 12:24 NIV). Often when one or both partners have experienced a loss of some kind, the sexual union presents an opportunity to comfort and relax one another. It is a time for the couple to pull together and experience the unity that they so desperately need. Losing a job, feeling stress from work, moving, having problems with children, and losing a loved one are times when comfort is desperately needed. And physical comfort, including holding, kissing, and even sexual union, can give care and warmth.

A wise couple will come together in physical and emotional unity during times of trial because such times naturally pull them apart. In His wisdom, God knows this is a danger point and therefore takes care to draw the couple back together tenderly and patiently.

Truth 10: Sexual Attitudes of Parents Are Transferred to Children

Children should learn that sex was created for the marriage relationship alone. This training should not start in the teenage years, but as early as nine or ten years old. Sexual intimacy was created as a gift from God to allow two people to express marital unity.

It is no accident that a whole book is devoted to the sexual and romantic life of a married couple in the Word of God. The very last chapter of the Song of Solomon ends with an admonition concerning sex and children. The Shulammite's brothers greet her and Solomon as they return home for a visit. The brothers ask about their younger sister who has yet to reach puberty, and discuss her character development in the area of sexual values. "If she is a wall, we shall build on her a battlement of silver; but if she is a door, we shall barricade her with planks of cedar" (Song of Solomon 8:9). "A wall" indicates strength, suggesting strong convictions and determination in abstaining from sexual relationship. "A door" indicates easy entry, or being sexually promiscuous.Significantly the bride responds by saying "I was a wall" (verse 10); she remained a virgin until her wedding day.

If you observe your teens to be walls, firmly resisting sexual temptations, reward them with more freedom. However, if they appear to be doors, open to pressures from friends, you are to lovingly put more fences around them to insure their protection from early experimentation. It is important that the older children assist the parents by being examples in the protection of the siblings. Some children need more boundaries than others. Observant parents will communicate readily with each child concerning sexuality values.

Throughout the Song of Solomon the phrase appears, "Do not arouse or awaken my love until she pleases" (Song of Solomon 2:7; 8:4; see also 3:5). According to these verses, no one should open himself or herself to arousal before the time of marriage fulfillment. Early teens should be taught the importance of avoiding tempting situations that can lead to such arousal. Constant communication as they grow to adulthood is not optional, but crucial. Pray continually for the Lord's protection for each child.

The sex talks we had with our children started when they were about eight or nine years old. Dating was not allowed until age sixteen and that was group dating. We communicated very thoroughly with our children all the way through junior high school, high school, and college. Open communication and asking the right questions along the way encouraged them to wait for marriage to have sex.

To a large degree, children learn from the attitudes of their parents. Deuteronomy 6 states that parents teach by what they do and say. Your convictions and actions play a major role in raising children. What you model to them becomes their strongest impression of sexual love.

Attitudes are also communicated by the parents' behavior. Research indicates that children learn very little from what you say and a great deal more from what you do. If Mom and Dad are not excited about each other, the children will miss the most important illustration of what love and marriage are all about. Couples may think they can subtly hide their attitudes from their children. Not so. If a father doesn't have a loving relationship with his wife, it could affect his daughter's concepts of femininity, and her future role in marriage. If the father doesn't have a good relationship with his daughter, it could affect her relationship with her future husband. This is also true of the father-son relationship, and the son's concepts of being a godly father and husband.

In summary, all these ten truths from God's Word teach one thing: *Sexual relations were created by God and He wants His children to enjoy His good gift!* Sex in marriage should be a pleasurable expression of a faith relationship. It is altogether good for us.

THIRTEEN

Naked and Unashamed

$\mathcal{T}$wo chapters on the sexual relationship! Isn't that a bit too much in a Christian book about unity in marriage?" If those are your thoughts, we can understand. But the physical union in marriage, and the physical pleasures that precede it, are a vital part to the emotional and spiritual unity that God ordained in marriage.

The first couple "were not ashamed," even though "they were both naked" (Genesis 2:25 KJV). Yet many Christian couples are uncomfortable or unsure about their sexual expression in marriage. Part of that is due to the curse of sin and the distortion of sex by our media. But some of the awkwardness comes from not learning about God's plan for marriage sexuality from the pulpit. That's understandable. Many pastors don't deal with the topic as openly as they would like because they have mixed audiences, including children.

Another reason for the awkwardness about sex arises from not knowing about differing sexual needs between women and men. This chapter will look at those differences and encourage wives and husbands to focus on meeting their spouse's needs.

God purposefully made women's sexual needs and motivations different than men's. Over a period of time, these differences reveal a great deal about the total relationship of the couple. The couple who is experiencing an agape marriage relationship will begin to see these differences as opportunities to serve and broaden the sexual experience.

As we look at the different motivations, remember that knowing your spouse's motivation for romance and responding to his or her sexual needs can benefit your whole relationship.

DIFFERING MOTIVATIONS FOR ROMANCE

Sexual Motivation for Women

Women are motivated greatly by the emotional dimension of their sexual relationships. Romantic love and feminine needs cannot be separated. Tender moments that communicate admiration and respect help to prepare wives for an exciting sexual experience. In fact, in the absence of romantic tenderness and emotional appreciation, wives sometimes enter the sexual union with feelings of "being used."

Women also are motivated by thoughts of a deep intimacy, of which the physical union is but one expression. Therefore, wives appreciate tender expressions, both verbally and physically. Women enjoy tenderness before, during, and after the sexual experience. Men, holding your wife after a sexual encounter is probably the most vital gift you can give to her. Sensitive communication about matters other than sex for twenty minutes before or after sex does a great deal to demonstrate your love. Doing so shows that you care about *her*, not just sex.

Many women tend to be cyclical in their sexual desire. That is, their desire tends to rise, then drop for several days after a sexual experience, only to rise again later. Women tend to be excited gradually and respond to tender touches and caresses. Privacy and a non-threatening environment are important to helping her release her emotions. Sensitive verbalization can soothe and motivate her.

Sexual Motivation for Men

In contrast, *men are motivated much more by the physical dimension* of their relationship. Normally, a man can struggle with a problem all evening and still be tremendously attracted to his wife's body. His sex drive is not cyclical, but continual. Tim LaHaye mentions several related issues in his book, *The Act of Marriage*. A man's sex drive is connected to his ability "to be the aggressor, provider, and leader of his family. The woman who resents her husband's sex drive while enjoying his aggressive leadership had better face the fact that she cannot have one without the other."[1]

Men usually respond spontaneously and instantaneously to physical stimuli. They are as likely to be stimulated through the eye as much as the touch. A man normally likes to caress his wife in the light, so he can see her clearly. Men are excited much more quickly than women, and distractions usually don't bother them. They experience immediate release in their sexual orgasm and may fall asleep immediately thereafter. With some effort on their part, however, they too can greatly enjoy those moments after intercourse, which are extremely important to their wives.

Few things in life give a man more a sense of having finished a task well than satisfying his wife sexually.

Few things in life give a man more a sense of having finished a task well than satisfying his wife sexually. To him, it is like wrapping up a package and tying a ribbon around it. The sexual dimension of marriage is so exhilarating, relaxing, and fulfilling.

Couples should never allow resentment to build toward one another in regard to these differences. Understand them, anticipate them, and work with them. A creative plan can turn these differences into real enjoyment. The woman who understands a man's natural, God-given sexual drive is overwhelmed when he tenderly meets her needs in spite of his own natural desires.

HELPING YOUR MATE
TOWARD SEXUAL ONENESS

Expressing sexual love changes all through marriage, including

early experimentation in marriage, hormonal and physical changes during pregnancy and nursing, years with small children with little time for privacy, the middle years, and finally the older years—each stage of life presents different sexual expressions. Yet, lovemaking during all these seasons can be extremely satisfying. All the changes that take place can be beautiful tests of your mutual and enduring love. Because life is always changing, so will your sexual experiences. Enjoy the changes, experiment, and communicate. Remember, through sexual oneness a husband and wife sometimes best express their spiritual and emotional commitments to each other.

Most sexual problems develop because of ignorance in the early years of marriage. Couples will ask advice on buying a house or car, or perhaps the discipline of their children. Few will seek help on the sexual relationship. Yet helping your spouse to desire and enjoy sexual oneness is important to having a healthy marriage. We encourage couples to read together Christian books on sex[2] and to seek counsel when problems persist over several months.

Here is some advice to married men and women from thirty years of our counseling experience.

Advice to Men

Men, your responsibility is to love your wife sacrificially as your own body. (See Ephesians 5:25, 28.) If you relate to her in a godly manner, you will enjoy a rewarding sexual relationship. Sacrificial love will pay great dividends for the rest of your life. Here are some simple guidelines.

Acceptance and communication. In the Scriptures, God instructs you to be excited and satisfied with your wife's body. Make it a point to tell her how you are drawn to her body. Fall in love with her so completely that you will not be affected by the inevitable changes produced by having children and aging. Convince your wife of your love and appreciation of her body. The man who fails to explicitly do this will eventually discover that she begins to hide her body from him. The result will be devastating. A husband has the power to make or break his wife's self-image concerning her body. The mirrors in your house and the young bodies pictured in advertisements all remind your wife that her looks are fading. Only you can convince her she still is pleasing to you physically and emotionally.

Good communication includes knowing your wife's fears and frustrations. A husband must take responsibility for helping his wife understand her sexual frustrations. Wives who develop sexual anxiety may not be initially aware of it. Insecurities about her appearance, the size of her breasts, her thighs, her stomach, or whatever, can cause a wife to lose her desire for sexual intimacy.

Husbands are to "live with [their] wives in an understanding way," according to 1 Peter 3:7. Your communication and reassurance are vital if you hope to keep your wife from labeling herself as unattractive. Never communicate, either through words or innuendo, that she needs to lose a few pounds or that she should have surgery in any given area of her body. She will be devastated by such insensitive comments and may never get over them.

Loving actions. Since so much of a woman's sexual enjoyment is tied to her emotional preparation, the husband must be prepared to take charge of easing his wife's burdens. A messy house, unattended children, uncertainty of personal attractiveness, criticism from her husband, and social pressures are typical problems that keep wives from releasing themselves emotionally. For example, an effective husband may get up on Saturday morning and let his wife sleep in. He dresses and feeds the children and helps clean the house. He may also take the children for several hours that afternoon so she can have her hair done or go shopping, enabling his wife to relax.

Such loving actions unburden a wife emotionally, which in turn allow her to become more aware of the husband's need.

When we first married, I used to blame Sally when she was not "up" sexually. Now I blame myself. I usually have not been romantically creative, or have not been sensitive to her needs. Sometimes such love will need to be sacrificial, inconvenient, or even difficult for the man. But the husband will do it because in his love he wants to please his wife and ease her burden.

A relaxing, pleasant environment. Men, protect your wife from sexual anxiety. This may seem obvious, but never take your cleanliness for granted! Brush your teeth and take a shower. Do things that take the pressure off the sexual union. Hot baths, rubdowns, and walks together just prior to intimate involvement foster communication and associate pleasure with sexual experiences. Candlelight and soft music reduce anxiety and help your wife to be uninhibited. Holding her and taking time to talk to her before sex add definite pleasurable associations with the act itself.

No man can guarantee a woman's sexual response every time, but he can create a satisfying experience for both of them most of the time.

Don't allow your wife to endure sexual pain! Occasional momentary pain upon entry is not abnormal, but if pain persists, seek medical help together. Rashes, infections, or more severe problems such as endometriosis can cause pain. Manual stimulation for both the man and woman gives pleasure and may alleviate tension or rejection brought on by painful intercourse. If these problems persist for an extended time in spite of proper medical help, seek counsel immediately.

Natural motivation. When a marriage is functioning according to God's perspective, women can be as sexually responsive as men. Unfortunately, outside pressures may frequently inhibit emotional responsiveness of women. On the other hand, men may not be as affected sexually by outside pressures. The following discussion, though addressed to men, can also help women, as husbands and wives learn to balance each other's sexual needs.

In most men and women, the level of sexual aggressiveness is natural, somewhat predictable. The following line represents the total spectrum of all natural sexual drives.

Not
Naturally   Naturally
Aggressive   Aggressive

|——————————|——————————|

Most women tend to be to the *left* of center (not naturally aggressive), while most men tend to be *right* of center (naturally aggressive). In other words, most women don't initiate sexual activity as often as men. These women may not be against sex, or even uninterested. They simply may not naturally think aggressively about sex.

190

However, apart from being properly approached, they may not develop an internal need for sexual fulfillment but every five to fifteen days. If properly motivated and stimulated by their husbands, they would be open to more frequent sexual advances.

Tragically, many husbands interpret this lack of natural aggression by their wives as failure or lack of interest. That's a big mistake. It simply may be a symptom of needed communication and support. The level of her natural aggressiveness should not be a measure of a husband's sexual failure or success. This natural aggressiveness has nothing to do with the couple's ultimate fulfillment.

Men must realize that God created their natural aggressiveness for obvious procreation purposes. It's OK for you to be the aggressor most of the time. It doesn't mean there is anything wrong with your wife. However, if a husband desires sex far too often for the wife, there may be a problem with communication, or feelings of rejection. These feelings can stem from his past. If a wife's sexual aggressiveness is lower than desired, the couple simply needs a mutually satisfying plan to change the balance. Counsel and openness can accomplish the solution to either of these problems.

In our culture, it is not unusual to find men who are less aggressive than their wives. Do not attach one another with labels that destroy emotional security. This will only worsen the problem. For husbands and wives, the solution is the same: Seek godly counsel.

Advice to Women

Enjoying sex. When we first married, I (Don) thought if I could just have my sexual needs met I would be happy. Before long I realized that the greatest need I had was not my own enjoyment, but my wife's. Sexually speaking, the greatest gift a woman can give to her husband is enjoying her own sexual experience. This is very motivating to a husband.

Too many wives look at sex merely as their duty to satisfy their husband's needs. Every woman should know that God wants her to feel good and to enjoy sex. If a wife has the freedom to look at her physical union as an enjoyable experience, her attitude will change tremendously. In order to enjoy the sexual union and to reach or-

gasm, *most women need to concentrate on their own bodies,* while the man enjoys concentrating and thinking about her body.

For maximum enjoyment, a wife needs a positive attitude concerning sex and marriage based on the Scriptures. She also needs to sense personal freedom in several areas, including (1) good communication with her mate, (2) satisfaction with her mate, (3) respect from and for her husband, (4) freedom to discover what feels good, (5) freedom to verbalize enjoyment, feelings, instructions, and (6) assurance that her husband will sensitively approach her, with her needs being his first priority. In addition, as we noted earlier, the woman will need to feel relaxed from her daily responsibilities, secure in her sexual setting, and secure that her body is attractive to her mate. She will also want personal cleanliness for herself and her husband.

Being feminine. God gave men a tremendous desire to pursue and serve their wives. In the natural sense, this drive manifests itself through sexual attraction. Wives should take advantage of this God-created desire instead of resenting it. Rather than condemn him, learn to motivate him and enjoy his instinctive desire.

How you dress is very important to him. Most men like their wives to wear feminine clothing as much as possible. Nice feminine undergarments are extremely motivating to husbands. Makeup and perfume can also affect his natural desire. Ask your husband what he enjoys about your clothing, or what he would like you to change.

Most men do not want their wives to be alluring to other men, so watch how short or tight fitting your skirts are. He may want you to wear particular outfits for him on occasion, but take care to be very modest in public.

FULL SEXUAL EXPRESSION

Again, because of the influences of our culture, wives and husbands often focus on sexual intercourse as the sole goal of sexual expression. Yet full sexual expression consists of much more than the physical union of husband and wife. Here are four aspects of the sexual relationship that contribute to a fulfilling sexual encounter between husband and wife.

A Focus on Your Mate's Total Person

Each couple should place the focus of their sexual relationship on being naked and unashamed instead of just having an orgasm in intercourse. While orgasm is a very important icing on the cake, it is not the cake. No couple can be assured of a successful orgasm experience every time, but every couple can be assured of a successful intimate experience. Characterize your physical lovemaking by focusing on each mate's total person.

Our caution is: Do not limit your sexual experiences to just intercourse. Many couples confine their sexual expression to fifteen quick minutes of intercourse. Couples who allow their sexual experience to dwindle to this point have, many times, guaranteed that the wife will have lower enjoyment for several reasons. Research shows that there is a large possibility that intercourse alone will not produce an orgasm for the wife. Second, fifteen-minute "quickies" foster servitude feelings in wives, not encouragement. They are very likely to feel used. Third, fifteen minutes does not allow wives to experience a total-person encounter. A naked and unashamed experience can take up to an hour. A women needs time to be reassured, to be listened to, to have her hurts mended, as well as to give her body time to prepare.

A women needs time to be reassured,

to be listened to, to have her hurts mended,

as well as to give her body time to prepare.

What are we saying? Husbands, you need to level the playing field! You can normally have an orgasm over 90 percent of the time. But quick lovemaking may limit her to orgasm to, at best, 40 percent of the time. You may be angry with God for not giving you a more sexually aggressive wife, but you may have failed repeatedly in the sensitivity and creativity department.

Guys, wake up! If you take time to deeply engage your wife's emotions, she will enjoy the sexual encounter even if she cannot have an orgasm. Cake is good, even without the icing. Do not allow your wife just to serve your needs. If she is at all frustrated, *both* of you must seek counsel. If this applies to you, don't expect a four- or five-day recovery. It may take months to repair as her trust in you grows.

Body Freedom

Since the sexual relationship involves a physical act, it is very important for partners to be excited about their mate's body as well as their own. Research indicates that sexual feelings intensify when couples are open and creative with each other's bodies. The woman who can uninhibitedly open her mind, body, and body movements to her husband's rhythm and motion will certainly experience increased enjoyment and success.

Today, it is common for a man to be attracted to his wife's body and even to express that verbally. It's not so common for a wife to express her appreciation for her husband's body. It is helpful for wives to reprogram their minds through Scripture by reading the Song of Solomon. For instance, consider Solomon's Shulammite wife, who said, "He is wholly desirable. This is my beloved and this is my friend" (Song of Solomon 5:16).

It is generally much easier for a husband to develop freedom with his body and with his mate's body. Generally, women are not so free. They tend to compare themselves with the youthful, unblemished bodies of models on TV, which can result in insecurity. Christian teaching has not helped women to be free with their husbands. Some women believe that the lower parts of their bodies are extremely unattractive and even unsanitary. This sets them up for sexual anxiety. Yet men, when polled on what part of their wife's body is most attractive, overwhelmingly said the lower parts. This is a shocking revelation to wives!

Because of these natural differences, husbands need to slow down and allow their wives time to adjust. With patience and sensitivity, after several months, the couple can learn to be open and free with one another's bodies. Once a wife experiences her husband's tenderness and patience, sex will become a more enjoyable experience for her.

Sexual Verbalization

As with all communication in marriage, sexual communication is a nonnegotiable. Talking about sexual excitement, instructions, hurts, fears, disappointments, joys, and anticipation are very important. The couple's ability to verbalize these to each other is imperative.

Several problems occur in sexual verbalization. It is not natural for men or women to verbalize during lovemaking for fear of losing their focus. Communicating criticism is easier than encouragement. "Don't do that," or "I don't like that," are said all too often instead of encouraging things like, "That feels good," or "One thing I love for you to do is . . ."

Because of the personal aspect of the sexual relationship, egos are easily injured. A mate who tries hard to please his partner, only to be criticized for his effort, may eventually stop trying. Hurt can turn a beautiful sexual experience into a bitter exchange of insults. Don't criticize *during* the physical act of lovemaking. If you have concerns, wait till the following day to discuss those issues. Approach the subject with humility and sensitivity and with much prayer.

Learning to verbalize can involve creating a sexual vocabulary. Sally and I conscripted terms from the Song of Solomon and developed words that we personally felt comfortable with. We laughed a lot and had a good time developing our intimate vocabulary. After years of marriage, it is amazing how comfortable we are with our terminology. Read the Song of Solomon out loud to each other. Have the wife take the part of the Shulammite and the husband, Solomon. You will laugh at some of the terminology, but you will begin to feel natural using sexual terms from this book. It is a beautiful poetic book and needs to be read often by couples.

Time Priority

Sexual freedom and blessing should increase the longer you're married. Moderate your past disappointments by considering the following fail-safe plan that changes your time priorities.

First, have a two-hour sexual experience weekly for the rest of your marriage. Schedule it if you have to, but make it happen. Plan an evening with no TV and without the children (or wait till they have gone to bed). You will be surprised at how creative you will become with your two-hour encounter.

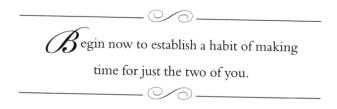

egin now to establish a habit of making

time for just the two of you.

The second commitment is very important as children come along. We suggest to couples that they take a twenty-four-hour time period alone together once a month. You can takes turns watching children with another couple who are doing the same thing. It's fun to sometimes have breakfast in bed, or sleep late, or have an early morning love-in. Be creative!

If a couple takes a night each week and a day every month to concentrate on their physical and emotional needs, most problems can be conquered together. Obviously, accomplishing this faithfully in the real world is hard. Yet, if you only take *half* of these days during the year, you will still characterize your sex life as being very satisfying. Begin now to establish a habit of making time for just the two of you. Your children will grow up and characterize your marriage as great. They will sense that you enjoy spending time together and that you love each other. That is the greatest gift you can give one another and your children.

WHAT ABOUT SEX IF YOU'RE ENGAGED?

Many counselors and well-meaning friends contend that premarital sex releases people from their inhibitions, strict morals, and religious hang-ups. If you are engaged and planning for a wedding, the commitment is there, and it's helpful to get to know each other, they say. Although we agree that certain hang-ups need emotional understanding, premarital sex is not the answer. Rather than freeing couples, premarital sex does just the opposite. It adds emotional pressure and puts you in bondage. It can rob you of the ability to clearly see God's will for marriage.

God's will is for sexual expression to occur only in the committed bonds of marriage. To God, sexual love expresses the more important spiritual commitment and unity between two married people. Sexual love, apart from marriage, reduces sex to a purely physical experience.

Some readers who are engaged have had premarital sex—perhaps you are involved in it right now. Recognize that it is sin. God didn't tell you to avoid premarital sex because He wanted to take away your fun. He has said no because He loves you and has a better way. If you have had premarital sex, I strongly encourage you to see a Christian counselor to help you seek God's forgiving perspective and to provide accountability.

Recognize that sin is forgivable regardless of the form it takes and that you need to ask God's forgiveness. If you are presently involved in premarital sex, you must now make a decision of your will to refrain. This will ensure a much better transition into marriage.

---

*E*xpress your excitement for future marital love. . . .

A brief statement, communicated sincerely, can meet

the need of being recognized and appreciated sexually.

Because of our human makeup and the cultural fantasy that is perpetrated on couples today, sexual involvement before marriage causes an unnatural emotional response. An air of false excitement and expectancy alters the normal marital sexual response. Therefore, a couple involved prior to marriage may have problems adjusting when this false expectancy is removed after the wedding. Stopping now will allow God to begin to give you an anticipation of a sexual relationship in marriage that is free from guilt and open to godly expression.

Here are some practical ideas that will help with this struggle. First, make a spiritual and verbal commitment together to stop your premarital sexual activities. Men, take the leadership in this decision. Women are as responsible before the Lord as men, but God expects you to exhibit leadership. Your future wife will respect you even more for being strong here.

Here is an alternative to sexual involvement that has worked for many couples. Although actual sexual involvement frustrates a relationship, the real need is not sexual contact, but sexual recognition and communication. I suggest to couples that after making their commitment to stop all sexual involvement, they try the following. When you spend time together, just before you part, excuse yourselves from family or friends and privately kiss affectionately. Then both of you should express your excitement for future marital love. The statement should be brief and stated as unto the Lord. Yet it should be a complete expression of what you feel and need in general terms.

Either the man or the woman might say, "Darling, I want you to know that I am excited about giving myself to you after the wedding. You are so attractive to me. I am going to pray specifically tonight that God will cause me to be a great lover to you after we marry." I have found that a brief statement, communicated sincerely, can meet the need of being recognized and appreciated sexually. Creativity by both will aid the development of sexual verbalization.

The key to this project is to *attempt this communication just as the couple is parting.* The sexual battle is usually lost not at the point of contact but at the point of putting yourself in a tempting situation. A couple who plans a day at the apartment watching television is in trouble from the start. Be verbally creative in meeting the other's need for physical attention.

We do not recommend a long engagement period for obvious reasons. If the wedding is a year away, consider moving up the date a few months. Usually it does not take more than four to six months to plan a wedding. This may not be possible, but it is easier to refrain sexually for six months than a year. If you still struggle with sexual involvement after these suggestions, the next step is to make yourselves accountable to someone else. Go together to a godly person in your church whom you can trust. Communicate your frustrations and make a commitment to do what is asked of you. Usually this type of accountability will do the job. Premarital counseling is a must if you desire for your marriage to have a good beginning.

Most importantly, remember that God created sex to be a very vital, fulfilling aspect of married life. Trust Him that He wants you to be more fulfilled than you even desire for yourself.

NOTES

1. Tim and Beverly LaHaye, *The Act of Marriage* (Grand Rapids: Zondervan, 1976), 22.

2. We recommend the following four books on the sexual relationship, each written from a Christian perspective: Ed and Gaye Wheat, *Intended for Pleasure* (Grand Rapids: Baker, 1981); Linda Dillow and Lorraine Pintus, *Intimate Issues* (Colorado Springs, Waterbrook, 1999); Tim and Beverly La Haye, *The Act of Marriage* (Grand Rapids, Zondervan, 1976); and Clifford and Joyce Penner, *The Gift of Sex* (Waco, Tex.: Word 1981).

FOURTEEN

Financial Freedom

*Y*ears ago, Susan, recognized as a spiritual leader in our community, gave us an unexpected call. She had had major financial problems, and as her story unfolded, I (Sally) was surprised by how much financial stress she lived with. Through bitter tears, Susan revealed the disappointment and resentment that had built up over the years regarding her husband's financial habits. She had prayed and prayed, but she could not resist resentment in this area.

Her husband habitually let bills become past due before paying them. When they arrived in the mail, he would pay them—months later! All of this came to a head one day when she was shopping, unfortunately with three friends. She attempted to charge a dress and was refused because of their payment record. She was extremely embarrassed and humiliated, and decided to seek counsel immediately.

Susan was a godly wife, yet her story taught us the dangers to a marriage of poor or absent financial planning. Financial stress is a major problem in most marriages. Frequently couples spend restless nights over financial fears. Howard Dayton, president and founder of

Crown Ministries, and Larry Burkett, president and founder of Christian Financial Concepts, agree that money-related issues are the number one cause instigating divorce. Indeed, 50 percent of couples who divorce cite finances as a major cause of disagreement. Few things generate more bitterness and resentment than money management.

Paul was certainly correct when he said to Timothy: "For the love of money is a root of all sorts of evil, and some by longing for it have wandered away from the faith and pierced themselves with many griefs" (1 Timothy 6:10).

The key phrase is *"some by longing for it."* The first financial problem to be solved in marriage is attitude. Jesus taught, "For where your treasure is, there your heart will be also"(Matthew 6:21). What role does money play in your marriage? Is it a blessing from God or a source of strife and division? Can you trust God even if you have little money? Every couple needs to agree on some financial absolutes to minimize attitude problems. Mature, solid marriages exhibit a balance of both biblical attitudes and financial discipline. Some couples have great attitudes, but still become financially strapped because they fail to anticipate, record, and control their budget.

Financial responsibility requires proper attitudes and faithful control. Problems occur when our worldly desires conflict with God's perspective. The following chart illustrates how our culture subtly says one thing about financial responsibility, while God's Word says another.

A CONTRAST IN PERSPECTIVES

Our Culture's View	**God's Perspective**
1. Fix your attention on money and possessions.	"But seek first His kingdom and His righteousness, and all these things will be added to you" (Matthew 6:33).
2. Wealth and possessions determine happiness in life.	"Beware, and be on your guard against every form of greed; for not even when one has an abundance does his life consist of his possessions" (Luke 12:15).

3. I'll be satisfied when I have more _____.

"He who loves money will not be satisfied with money, nor he who loves abundance with its income." (Ecclesiastes 5:10).

4. A man's wealth is his security.

"God is our refuge and strength, a very present help in trouble. Therefore we will not fear, though the earth should change, and though the mountains slip into the heart of the sea" (Psalm 46:1–2).

5. Financial success is the first priority.

Matthew 6:33 (above); also, "Not addicted to wine or pugnacious, but gentle, peaceable, free from the love of money" (1 Timothy 3:3).

You might be tempted to read quickly over these conflicting statements without a lot of personal conviction, but don't! Any person who has grown up in America cannot help but be influenced by our culture's thought patterns. The resulting pressures and conflicts are painful. The more couples follow God's thought patterns, the more freedom and blessing they will experience.

FINANCIAL FAITHFULNESS

To develop God's perspective on finances, first look at the example of Christ Himself. Jesus indicated that financial faithfulness is a thermometer of our relationship with God.

"He who is faithful in a very little thing is faithful also in much; and he who is unrighteous in a very little thing is unrighteous also in much. Therefore, if you have not been faithful in the use of unrighteous wealth, who will entrust the true riches to you? And if you have not been faithful in the use of that which is another's, who will give you that which is your own? No servant can serve two masters; for either he will hate the one, and love the other, or else he will be devoted to one, and despise the other. You cannot serve God and wealth." (Luke 16:10–13)

Jesus compared money to a "little thing." He made it clear that in comparison to the important things in life, money is a small item. But this *little thing* is a big indicator of a man's faithfulness in serving God. The way a man handles his finances is a strong indicator of his trustworthiness as a person. Jesus asked (verse 11) how God could give His servants true riches if they could not be trusted financially. "The true riches" refers to the grace, hope, and peace that God gives to a person or couple who adheres to His perspective. Today, men crave money to find peace, but God says money does not bring peace or contentment.

Jesus said that every person is either trusting God or trusting in the security of money. Which do you trust as a person or couple? Couples who apply faith in finances experience blessing and peace. Couples who put their hope in money and possessions, however slightly, will struggle greatly. Often the struggle results in questioning God or feeling depressed. There is seldom any middle ground. We are convinced that God uses finances as few other things to teach dependence upon Him.

To find God's perspective on money, consider the following truths. Accepting these four perspectives will do more to insure financial peace of mind than anything the world can provide.

FOUR PILLARS OF FINANCIAL MATURITY

1. Ownership

Interestingly, I (Don) began to feel a compulsion to own things *the minute* I bought my first car. This compulsion forced me to compare myself with others who owned more, and I became discontent. Indeed, the advertising industry attempts to accomplish one thing: to make us dissatisfied with what we have. Advertisers tell us that their products will make us happier, whether the item is a house, car, stereo, or simply toothpaste. If their claims were true, there would be a lot of satisfied people in this country; but just the opposite is true. We always seem to want more. The Scriptures challenge that desire.

King David, a man after God's own heart (1 Samuel 13:14; Acts 13:22), knew that true riches are found in knowing and giving to the mighty God.

> "Yours, O Lord, is the greatness and the power and the glory and the victory and the majesty, indeed everything that is in the heavens and the earth; Yours is the dominion, O Lord, and You exalt Yourself as head over all. Both riches and honor come from You, and You rule over all, and in Your hand is power and might; and it lies in Your hand to make great and to strengthen everyone. Now therefore, our God, we thank You, and praise Your glorious name. But who am I and who are my people that we should be able to offer as generously as this? For all things come from You, and from Your hand we have given You. For we are sojourners before You, and tenants, as all our fathers were; our days on the earth are like a shadow, and there is no hope. O Lord our God, all this abundance that we have provided to build You a house for Your holy name, it is from Your hand, and all is Yours." (1 Chronicles 29:11–16)

The Scriptures declare that God is head over all and that all things come from Him. We are simply stewards of God's possessions for a short time, and we are to worship and glorify Him with what He has given us. When others are in need, God desires that we should be free to give from our abundance. Sally and I often discuss how God uses the possessions He has given us to test us. God just wants to know if we see ourselves as *owners* or only *stewards* of His possessions.

Our first test came early in our marriage following the purchase of a brand-new washing machine. At the time, we were close friends with a couple in seminary who had very little money, and we told them they could wash their clothes in our machine. Every Saturday they came over to do laundry. Sally began to feel uneasy about this, thinking that the machine might break because of overuse, leaving us stuck with the repair bill. But we reminded ourselves that the machine was the Lord's and not ours. By faith, we had given all our possessions to Him to be used however He chose. As a result, we changed our attitude from one of possessiveness to gratefulness, believing that God had blessed us with a machine that others could use. That machine lasted more than ten years. It was never repaired, and we later sold it in a garage sale. God faithfully takes care of all His possessions!

Sally and I don't struggle very long anymore with possessiveness. It seems the Lord always reminds us who gave it, who plans to use it, and who is going to pay the bills. And He reminds us who may even take it away! We continually give Him our lives, our possessions, our money, our children and families, and so on. He has repeatedly tested our hearts in giving. However, in return, He has given us peace and contentment, along with more material blessings than we could have ever dreamt. Being a steward is very freeing indeed. However, when we occasionally take ownership back, peace becomes elusive, our struggle returns, and God graciously reminds us of who owns it all.

According to Deuteronomy, these struggles help us to recognize our motives and test our obedience: "Remember how the Lord your God led you all the way . . . to humble you and to test you in order to know what was in your heart, whether or not you would keep his commands" (8:2 NIV).

2. God's Providence

Another constant struggle for Christians is that of comparing their financial resources to others. Feeling superior over those with less, or hating and resenting those with more can destroy God's perspective in your life. There is even a great tendency among some today to feel proud about their simple lifestyles. God clearly speaks about differences in financial situations.

> But you, why do you judge your brother? Or you again, why do you regard your brother with contempt? For we will all stand before the judgment seat of God. For it is written, "As I live," says the Lord, "Every knee shall bow to Me, and every tongue shall give praise to God." So then each one of us will give an account of himself to God. Therefore let us not judge one another anymore (Romans 14:10–13).

> "The Lord makes poor and rich; He brings low, He also exalts. He raises the poor from the dust, He lifts the needy from the ash heap to make

them sit with nobles, and inherit a seat of honor; for the pillars of the earth are the Lord's, and He set the world on them." (1 Samuel 2:7–8)

God leaves no doubt on this issue: *He* makes both rich and poor. There are no accidents in business. Whatever your state, God put you there, not luck or breaks. We have all seen sure deals collapse and totally hopeless deals pay tremendous financial dividends. Don't waste your time blaming or watching others, because the one to look to is Christ Himself. It is not man, but God, who causes all things to happen.

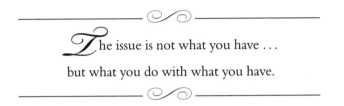

The issue is not what you have . . .

but what you do with what you have.

The issue is not what you have or don't have, but what you do with what you have. You are accountable to God for what He has given you. God's ultimate purpose is to conform us to the image of His Son, Jesus Christ, and He uses finances to shape us. Can you thank Him at all times for what you have or don't have? Everything we have is a gift from Him, and is a part of His plan for our lives.

3. Contentment

So, if we do not really own anything, and God is the one who makes rich or poor, what should be our attitude? Apart from basic food and clothing, we must recognize that there is no real hope in things—there is only the *appearance* of hope. So be content with food and clothing if that's all you have.

As Paul wrote, "For we have brought nothing into the world, so we cannot take anything out of it either. If we have food and covering, with these we shall be content." He then warned, "But those who want to get rich fall into temptation and a snare and many foolish and harmful desires which plunge men into ruin and destruction" (1 Timothy 6:7–9). The writer of Hebrews also wrote, "Make sure that your character is free from the love of money, being content with what you have; for He Himself has said, 'I will never desert you, nor will I ever forsake you'" (13:5).

If you have wealth, or desire it, then you must be very cautious. Remember that God is still responsible for meeting your needs. "He Himself has said, 'I will never desert you, nor will I forsake you.'" Trust Him to meet your needs. He has promised to do so; and in many cases He has given us many of our wants as well. And consider this insight from wise King Solomon. "Give me neither poverty nor riches; feed me with the food that is my portion, that I not be full and deny You and say, 'Who is the Lord?' or that I not be in want and steal, and profane the name of my God" (Proverbs 30:8–9).

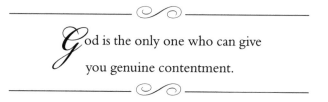

God is the only one who can give you genuine contentment.

It is human nature to always want more. God is the only one who can give us genuine contentment. As hard as it is to grasp, you must realize the difference between needs, wants, and desires, and claim God's promises to meet your needs. The ability to be content in these promises is a major ingredient in God's recipe for financial maturity. Throughout your married life, you will experience times of real financial need. Such times offer wonderful opportunities to acknowledge your needs to God, ask Him to meet those needs, and then watch Him answer.

There is such contentment and joy in answered prayer! Over many years Sally has kept a careful journal of prayers and answers to prayer. Our faith has grown tremendously as we read of God's past faithfulness. This gives us faith as we face the future. Our children also learned the faithfulness of God because we often recounted ways in which He met the family's needs. Now, as adults, they do not doubt His care for us.

Paul wrote that Christians should let God know needs and wants. "Be anxious for nothing, but in everything by prayer and supplication with thanksgiving let your requests be known to God. And the peace of God, which surpasses all comprehension, will guard your hearts and your minds in Christ Jesus" (Philippians 4:6–7). These verses don't mean that God will give us your wants; but if He doesn't, He will give you His peace. And what more could you want than the peace of God, which surpasses your ability to comprehend ?

4. Security

The last pillar of God's perspective on finances is security. Real security is not found in the uncertainty of riches. Instead, security is found by fixing your hope on God, who gives you everything you need. Scripture abounds with this concept, both in finances and in human relationships. Paul wrote to Timothy: "Instruct those who are rich in this present world not to be conceited or to fix their hope on the uncertainty of riches, but on God, who richly supplies us with all things to enjoy. Instruct them to do good, to be rich in good works, to be generous and ready to share, storing up for themselves the treasure of a good foundation for the future, so that they may take hold of that which is life indeed" (1 Timothy 6:17–19).

If you place your hope and security in God to the point that you actually share with others, then God promises "life indeed." Faith is acting on a statement from God, even when it goes against human reason. Financial freedom and security are in God, not in earthly possessions.

These four pillars of financial freedom—ownership, God's providence, contentment, and security—give you the foundation to use money properly in your life. When you understand that His gracious hand has given all of your material goods, you will be more careful how you give, save, invest, and spend. Prayerfully, you will become faithful stewards of God's money and possessions.

UNDERSTANDING AND APPLYING:
Giving, Saving, Investing, and Spending

The four financial pillars are tested and proved in the practical financial activities of giving, saving, investing, and spending. Scripture instructs us in each of these important activities. Develop a careful strategy for each one.

Giving

The importance of giving financially to the church (or Temple in Old Testament times) and to others is a theme throughout Scripture. The Old and New Testaments give very specific direction on amounts to give, when to give, and to whom to give.

Paul instructed each believer to put aside money in order to give regularly, based on how much God has given you. (See 1 Corinthians 16:1–2.) We Christians are to set aside the money *before* we spend, or we won't have it to give. In the Old Testament, men gave 20 percent as required by the Law. If you lived in Israel, the 20 percent was divided between the government (under the rule of God) and the Temple (also under the rule of God). Thus, 10 percent went to the Lord's work, and 10 percent went to keep the government operating.

In the New Testament, we are to ask the Spirit of God to direct our giving. "Each one must do just as he has purposed in his heart" (2 Corinthians 9:7). For some, it will be 10 percent, some 20 percent, and some more. Give with a gracious spirit and not one of "compulsion, for God loves a cheerful giver" (verse 7). Curiously, surveys show that *the more* a couple earns, the more possessive and materialistic they become. Each couple should take seriously God's command to give liberally.

Why does God desire that we give generously? Giving is a redemptive act—God graciously and tenderly lets you help to meet the needs of others. Doing so forces your eyes off your needs and yourself. It allows you to keep the right perspective on who really owns your money, and who gives it. You will receive a blessing from God if you give sacrificially to others. I challenge you to let the Holy Spirit tell you what to give and to whom.

The Scripture instructs us to give to those who minister to us (Galatians 6:6). The ability of God's full-time servants to be available depends on our faithfulness to support them financially, be that in our local churches, Christian organizations, or missionary agencies. Above all, we are to be visionary in our giving. Trust the One who has given so much to you. God wants to use you as a reservoir to meet needs! Allow God to use you greatly so He can enlist you as a supplier for His work.

Giving triggers a blessing cycle: The more you give, the more

God gives. Jesus expressed it this way: "Give, and it will be given to you. They will pour into your lap a good measure—pressed down, shaken together, and running over. For by your standard of measure it will be measured to you in return" (Luke 6:38).

Even when you loan money to others, consider giving the money instead. Giving releases you from always wondering if the recipient will repay the loan. Loaning money can cause you to become resentful and bitter toward the person. I am not saying that a loan should not be repaid, but God says your contentment should not depend on another person's lack of responsibility. Always keep an open and giving spirit toward others. God does amazing work in our lives when we give unselfishly. (See the command to give generously in Deuteronomy 15:10–11.)

Beyond your regular tithing to the church and your offerings to the church and Christian organizations, here are some creative ways to give out of your abundance:

- Food: when someone is out of a job, has a baby, or has a death in the family
- Clothing: for others less fortunate or to mission organizations
- Furniture: for church people or young couples in need
- Cars: for a missionary or pastor who is in need
- Stock: given as a benefit to the recipient and you

Rather than selling your items, ask God to whom you should give it. Your part is to give and God's part is to bless.

Saving

Saving is vital to financial peace and joy. We often deal with couples struggling with debt, or those who have no money at the end of the month. A poor family with a little money in savings is much freer financially than a rich family who is overextended.

Scripture says there is wisdom in saving for future needs. According to Proverbs 21:20, "There is precious treasure and oil in the dwelling of the wise, but a foolish man swallows it up." Similarly,

Proverbs says concerning a father's savings, "A good man leaves an inheritance to his children's children, and the wealth of the sinner is stored up for the righteous" (13:22).

We encourage couples to begin a habit of saving, no matter how small the amount, even if it's only $50 a month. If you run out of money at the end of the month, the pressure is much less if you have an additional $500 in savings. A good rule of thumb is to save 10 percent of your salary each month. Saving, like giving, needs to come *before* and not after spending. If you begin saving when first married, you will be amazed how much you will accumulate for a home, college education, and emergencies. Money in savings can tide you over if a job is lost. Most Americans are one paycheck away from bankruptcy. Are you?

Investing

God's Word teaches key principles for making wise investments and saving. First, avoid get-rich-quick schemes. Build security slowly, Proverbs warns us (21:5; 28:22). We believe the best strategy is to put a little aside each pay period.

Second, do not have a strong desire to get rich, remembering Paul's warning, "But those who want to get rich fall into temptation and a snare and many foolish and harmful desires which plunge men into ruin and destruction" (1 Timothy 6:9). Obtain money by hard work, for "Wealth obtained by fraud dwindles, but the one who gathers by labor increases it" (Proverbs 13:11).

Third, always seek counsel from someone with successful experience. (See Proverbs 20:18.) Those who are older and more mature often have more wisdom. Don't be afraid to ask questions when it comes to investing. Find someone who will take the time to listen and help you create a plan. It is not wise to borrow against projected future income to make investments, or to cover expenditures in the present. Also, be careful about seeking counsel from someone who is selling an investment product or service. Their advice might be biased toward making the sale.

Finally, remember that security is not in wealth but in the gracious hand of God, who has ultimate control of our lives.

Come now, you who say, "Today or tomorrow we will go to such and such a city, and spend a year there and engage in business and make a profit." Yet you do not know what your life will be like tomorrow. You are just a vapor that appears for a little while and then vanishes away. Instead, you ought to say, "If the Lord wills, we will live and also do this or that." But as it is, you boast in your arrogance; all such boasting is evil. Therefore, to one who knows the right thing to do, and does not do it, to him it is sin. (James 4:13–17)

Uncontrolled Spending (Debt)

Debt has literally destroyed many marriages, and the national debt may lead our country to financial collapse. (See *The Coming Economic Earthquake* by Larry Burkett.) Though an improving economy at the end of the 1990s has lessened the debt somewhat, it remains a staggering $5.7 trillion. Debt is considered normal today, both on the national and personal level. Personal debt is at an all-time high, and personal bankruptcy filings "are expected to exceed two million by the year 2001."[1] According to the American Bankruptcy Institute, more than 90 percent of those bankruptcies will be the result of out-of-control credit card spending.[2]

Credit card debt is extremely stressful in marriage. Most financial problems occur in the spending area. "Americans spend on average $1.10 for every $1.00 they earn."[3] You should know at all times how much you owe so you won't go deeper into debt. And then begin to escape your credit card debt by paying off high interest cards first. Then commit to make purchases with cash. If you have credit cards, pay the balance each month so you don't accumulate debt. Limit yourself to two or three credit cards at the most.

Paul exhorts the Romans to "owe nothing to anyone except to love one another" (Romans 13:8). Although he was not speaking directly of finances, the application is valid.

Establish a budget to govern your purchases. If you don't do this, you will have problems in your marriage. Often two people come together in marriage with totally different ways of looking at spending. Pay off high monthly payments (car and house) as quickly as possible. When your car is paid off, resist the urge to buy a new car. Instead, put the same money in the bank for the purchase of a newer car when needed. Buying a newer car with limited mileage may be a better investment than a brand-new car. If you have a thirty-year loan on your house, begin paying an extra $100–150 a month toward the principle. You will be amazed at how fast the house gets paid off. Taking out a fifteen-year loan is better than a thirty-year loan because of the thousands of dollars of interest saved.

The following chart, "Questions to Ask Before Spending," is an example of the type of questions you might ask yourself to determine if your expenditures are in line with God's perspective. Study this with your spouse.

QUESTIONS TO ASK BEFORE SPENDING

Question	Scripture
1. Is my spending motivated by the love of money?	1 Timothy 6:9; 1 John 2:15
2. Has God already led me to meet a need with this money?	2 Corinthians 8:14
3. Do I have a doubt about it?	Romans 14:23
4. Have I given God an opportunity to use it?	Psalm 37:5; Proverbs 10:3
5. Will this spending hinder my spiritual growth?	1 Corinthians 6:12; Hebrews 12:1; 2 Corinthians 11:3
6. Is this spending a good investment?	Proverbs 20:14
7. Does it put me into debt?	Proverbs 22:7
8. Will it be meaningful to my family?	1 Timothy 3:4; 5:8

Each of these factors should be considered when making a financial decision. Wise counsel from another person helps. Couples who keep tight control over their purchases will have little trouble keeping God's perspective on money management. Peace and contentment will be their reward.

ABOUT A BUDGET

Any family that desires to get control of their finances should start by setting up a monthly budget. A budget is simply a projection of future income and expenses. A simple budget really does not take much time but, over a period of five to six months, can help a couple manage their finances. Typically the budget won't be absolutely accurate at first, but it should be reviewed and adjusted faithfully each month. The couple can then evaluate any problem areas together, find solutions, and adjust their spending patterns. Several good financial management books and computer programs are available. We highly recommend the resources of Christian Financial Concepts in Gainesville, Georgia.[4] Also, a twelve-week course on managing finances God's way has been produced by Crown Ministries in Longwood, Florida, and has changed the lives of thousands of couples.[5]

Couples are never more aware of their lack of oneness than when they are dealing with finances.

It is very important to compare your actual expenses each month with your budget. Then you can see exactly what you are spending and where you tend to overspend. A budget's value is realized as you continuously review and update it. Couples who plan usually tend to make do, and their money goes farther.

Couples are never more aware of their lack of oneness than when they are dealing with finances. Since each of you will have different ways of handling money, it is essential to discuss how you are going to approach financial problems. You must agree on your priorities for purchasing and establish your financial values. Apply the faith commitments of Genesis 1 and 2 to your finances. Agree together to transfer to the Lord all of your possessions. Conflict results when there is no mutual commitment or when one spouse acts independently from the other.

INDIVIDUAL RESPONSIBILITIES FOR FINANCES

Men have the primary responsibility for the financial integrity of the home. God has instructed husbands to provide for their families (1 Timothy 5:8), and He has never changed that mandate. The man is responsible to provide for the family's welfare through working, though the wife also may work. (A layoff or poor health may at times shift the responsibility to the woman.) The husband also has the chief responsibility to control the expenditures, pay the bills, initiate giving, and save for a rainy day. That does not mean he is smarter, more gifted, or even more successful at these things, but he is *primarily* responsible. With humility, take your leadership very seriously.

If your wife is more gifted than you are in the area of managing finances and desires to help, give her major responsibility. The husband still must bear the financial pressure, being sure there is enough to pay the bills and grow the savings, even as the wife does the bookkeeping. If the husband begins to hedge on his responsibility, however, or if the wife struggles, she should give the financial record keeping back to him.

Wives, you must be careful when you take such responsibility not to "put your husbands down" in their areas of weakness. Neither of you should belittle the other when it comes to money. Remember, you are "joint heirs" of the grace of life. If a couple communicates well in the area of finances, their marriage will exhibit peace.

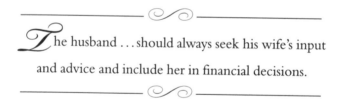

The husband . . . should always seek his wife's input and advice and include her in financial decisions.

Although the husband should take leadership with the family finances, he should always seek his wife's input and advice and include her in financial decisions. If the wife works outside the home, try not to become dependent on her income. It would be wise to invest her salary. This will allow you to set money aside for the future and it will also give your wife the potential to stop working if she so desires. It can give her more flexibility to respond to the needs of any children at home. Becoming too dependent on her salary will eventually affect how a mother cares for her children. Don't allow a desire for material things to compete with the needs of the children. After the children leave home, she may want to return to work. However, she should always be free to work or not to work.

Both the husband and wife should maintain a spirit of joy, freedom, and creativity in the household. Some people become extremely creative when they are low on money. They have joy in giving and yet have a tight budget. Refinishing furniture, selling crafts, having garage sales, and performing do-it-yourself repairs on the home are among the creative money savers that low-budget families adopt. When their circumstances are approached by faith, low-budget families can often be happier than couples who have more financial resources.

Most couples will struggle financially, especially early in marriage. It seems that God uses money more than anything else to teach dependence on Him. When you struggle, reread this chapter to review God's perspective, and the Holy Spirit will encourage and direct you.

NOTES

1. March 1998 study by the WEFA Group; the projected figure of 2.2 million bankruptcies by 2001 comes from Visa U. S. A., the credit card company, based on the WEFA report. See "2 Million Bankruptcies by 2001," 14 July 1998, at http://www.visa.com.
2. Elif Sinanoglu, "I Chucked My Credit Cards and Saved More Than $150 a Month," *Money*, August 1996, 64.
3. Larry Burkett, *Money Matters* Newsletter, April 1997, Christian Financial Concepts, Gainesville, Ga.
4. Contact Christian Financial Concepts at 1-800-722-1976.
5. Contact Crown Ministries at 1-407-331-6000.

FIFTEEN

Loving Those In-laws

*A*lthough in-law jokes are common, most couples fail to find this relationship amusing. Few fully realize the potential stress, anxiety, and hurt that can come if they are unprepared for potential in-law problems. To be forewarned is to be forearmed!

About the time wedding invitations are sent, wedding showers begin, and plans for the ceremony are under way, couples realize that parents usually have strong opinions about the wedding. By the time the wedding arrives, simple parent-child relationships may have turned into a complex minefield of disagreement and hurt. The bride cries, "Oh, why can't Mom understand?" and the groom wonders, "How did I upset them so much?" Caught off guard, the couple has unintentionally created a source of conflict that cuts deeply into the emotional needs of both the couple and their parents. Before they realize it, their in-laws have already developed opinions about their future son- or daughter-in-law.

The toughest aspect of preparing for a positive in-law relationship is you don't get a practice run! Your introduction to them can

be either tremendously personal and meaningful, or negative and hurtful. After all, the future of their son or daughter is at stake. Only after having children of our own have we understood this pressure. When our oldest daughter was only eight, Don began to realize that one day some guy would tell us he deserved our little girl. And sure enough, eighteen years later, he did! Fortunately, God was gracious in giving us a fine son-in-law. We know parents desire close relationships with their future sons- or daughters-in-law, but their initial introduction can sometimes be emotionally stressful on them.

Sometimes these introductions take place while planning the wedding. Other times couples have known each other a long time. In our transient society, it is common for a son or daughter to bring his or her future mate home just weeks or months before the wedding. Forcing two families who are usually complete strangers to come together amiably is not a natural thing. In fact, it is a miracle if it goes well.

DON'S IN-LAW BEGINNING

I can still remember meeting Sally's parents for the first time, *only one week before the wedding.* The reason was that we met and dated in a different state than Sally's home, and we were engaged within three months. Mom and Pop Hill are extremely likable people, and the slight problems we encountered were due to the awkward situation, and not them.

I arrived in Boulder, Sally's hometown, about 2 P.M. I had stopped earlier to clean up and put a suit on before meeting Sally's family. Since they lived in the mountains above Boulder, I decided to drop in on Sally's dad at work to get directions to their house. Pop was a well-known auto mechanic in Boulder. When I entered his shop, the supervisor told me Mr. Hill was working under a car, several cars down the line.

I was spotlessly dressed, overly aggressive, and somewhat nervous. I walked up to the car and said to his feet, which were sticking out, "Mr. Hill, I am Don Meredith." Stunned, Mr. Hill got about halfway out from under the car before I grabbed his greasy hand and said "Hello!" He was embarrassed about the grease, and we both felt rather awkward. He gave me directions to their house, and I left with my clean suit and greasy hand.

That night the pressure escalated. I quickly discovered that Sally's house had only one bathroom, and you had to go through her parents' bedroom to get there! After going to bed, my worst fears came true. I had to use the bathroom. I'm a very modest person. I waited as long as I could, and then I walked through their bedroom. I flushed the toilet and it sounded like Niagara Falls. I was so embarrassed! I felt emotional pressure from that point forward.

Later in the week we had a serious problem concerning the phone expenses. Sally and I had made some long-distance calls related to our wedding plans. However, we forgot to tell the Hills that we intended to pay for the calls. All the calls were long, full of questions, congratulations, and general catch-up, and they were all expensive. Finally, Sally mentioned her parents' concern over all the calls. This was perfectly understandable, but in light of the tension, I reacted strongly against Sally. I took pride in my financial responsibility and felt my integrity being questioned.

These problems sound foolish as I retell them, but at the time they were very serious. Four people, who under normal circumstances would have hit it off perfectly, started out on the wrong foot. Since then, things have smoothed out, and, by God's grace, our in-law problems have been minor. Our family greatly enjoys our times at Sally's parents' home, and we all look forward to our visits. This is true of my family as well.

Many couples start off wrong and are then burdened with poor in-law relationships for years. Once again, it will take faith to develop positive in-law relationships. For this reason, couples need to know what God says concerning in-laws.

LEAVING ONE'S FATHER AND MOTHER

God established His foundational thoughts concerning in-laws at the time He created marriage: "For this cause a man shall leave his father and his mother, and be joined to his wife; and they shall become one flesh" (Genesis 2:24). In this passage the man is commanded to leave upon marriage, yet throughout the Old Testament numerous examples are given of women leaving. The Hebrew word used in Genesis 2:24 for "leave" means to abandon or break off completely. God is saying that before a significant new relationship can

221

begin, the old parent-child relationship must cease. By this, God means that in issues of authority the parents no longer have responsibility.

After twenty or so years of responding to parental authority, there [is] a tendency to continue the dependence even after marriage.

God does not mean that the parental relationship should end altogether. Obviously, *children should never stop honoring their parents.* God is not against parents. His strong command to men and women is to put their full trust in God and their mates. Total mate satisfaction and respect can occur only when a couple has established a new primary allegiance.

God knew that after twenty or so years of responding to parental authority, there would be a tendency to continue the dependence even after marriage. Therefore, God indicates that one dependent relationship should end so that another can begin.

Although the parents' authority ends with the creation of the new relationship, the couple's responsibility to honor their parents continues. Deuteronomy 5:16 tells us that the duty of a child is to honor his parents. This word "honor" speaks primarily of valuing at a high price, showing deep respect or reverential awe. In marriage, parental experience and advice are very important. Still, decisions must be made by the couple apart from parental control. Even though parental advice may be necessary at times, it is better for the couple to go to the parents and not vice versa.

WAYS THAT COUPLES DON'T LEAVE

During our counseling, we have observed four common ways couples fail to leave their parents. These examples of failure to leave can be so subtle that couples may feel frustration without even understanding why.

1. *Parental Wealth and Social Benefits.* This problem reveals a conscious or subconscious dependence on parents for financial or social benefits to the point that the couple fails to acknowledge their own independence. For instance, a husband may allow his mother to criticize his wife so that the financial relationship with his parents won't be endangered. Other couples tend to spend too much time at the home of parents because of social or financial advantages. This dependence may hinder the development of the new relationship. This can be a two-way problem when some parents spend too much time with their children, often resulting in the in-law child resenting the new parents.

2. *Parental Model.* Some couples, again consciously or subconsciously, compare some area of their mate's performance to that of their parents. This comparison can ultimately cause dissatisfaction. I have seen men become completely disillusioned with their wives because they do not develop a particular housekeeping habit or cooking abilities that the husbands' mothers may have had. On the other hand, I have seen women lose respect for their husbands because they did not project the same financial stability as their fathers. These expectations are especially true in early marriage. Unfair comparisons like these can destroy marital oneness and commitment.

3. *Parental Approval.* Some mates remain dependent on their parents' approval after marriage due to an extremely strong or domineering parent. The need for parental approval may block trust in their new mate. Women have told me that they love their husbands, yet they perform to please their own mothers because they need Mom's approval. These new wives may be frustrated if their mothers disapprove of their husbands. They clean house the way Mom would want, discipline the children with Mom in mind, all the while hoping for her recognition or approval. Women who need approval in this way will jeopardize their husbands' sense of security and leadership. Similarly, men who are overly dependent on their father's approval can lower their wives' respect for them.

4. *Parental Relationship Substitute.* Nothing deflates a spouse more than for the mate to continue looking to their parents to meet primary emotional needs, especially when the spouse's own emotional needs go unmet as a result. We have counseled men and women who continue to call or go see their parents about most key issues in their lives, sometimes before they consult their mate. They give affection, receive most of their security, share their criticism, and even express most of their creative abilities with their parents. This behavior not only excludes their mates, but deeply hurts and divides them. It also creates confusion and a lack of dependence on the spouse.

HOW TO TRULY CLEAVE TO YOUR MATE

Failing to leave your parents hurts them in the long run as well as your mate and yourself. Agree together on a mutual plan to leave the authority of your parents. Here are several suggestions for truly leaving your parents' authority and cleaving to your spouse for help, comfort, and advice in decision making.

First, evaluate everyone's needs. Parents are not your enemy; they just do what comes naturally. If misunderstandings arise between you and your parents or parents-in-law, don't strike out at them for loving you, even if their method is wrong. Since both mates have an innate need to be at peace with their parents, don't be disrespectful to your in-laws.

Instead, when frustrations occur, analyze the situation with your mate and agree together about the cause. Evaluate everyone's real need, what went wrong, and most importantly, look for a *creative solution.* If either mate has wronged a parent, ask forgiveness. If a decision is needed to protect the integrity of the marriage, make it together. Then look for a creative way to communicate this to the parents.

Second, maintain privacy. Commit together never to share any intimate needs or decisions with either set of parents without your mate's permission. A husband may be dreaming of a new car, and his wife simply mentions it to her dad. The father then voices his disapproval to her husband, and the husband feels betrayed. Couples must build their lives together, and everything should remain private unless agreed otherwise.

Third, handle critical statements with care. Never be critical about your mate to your parents or allow them to make critical statements about your mate. Sharing something critical about your mate is damaging, not only to your mate, but also to your parents. Why? Because parents never forget the problems shared, and rarely allow your mate to change (in their minds). Your parents naturally become overly protective of their own children. We know one wife who revealed a financial irresponsibility by her mate in the first year of their marriage, and her parents are still bringing it up after twenty years. Parents don't have the opportunity to see your mate change and improve as you do. They only have your comments to go on.

Do yourself and your parents another favor. The next time they make a critical statement about your mate, respond with a strong but loving rebuff. I know of one man whose mother was just leading up to a critical remark about his wife. He interrupted with, "Mom, I love you a lot, but please don't be critical of my wife. I want you to know she is God's gift to me, and I don't want to hear those criticisms."

His mother hastily replied, "Don't be silly; I wasn't going to be critical of her."

The wise son responded with, "Forgive me, Mom. I just so want you two to be friends, because I love you both so much." He was strong but kind to his mother.

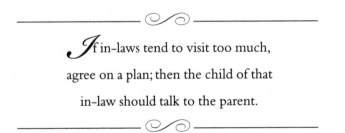

If in-laws tend to visit too much,
agree on a plan; then the child of that
in-law should talk to the parent.

Fourth, develop a plan for visiting in-laws. Before visiting your parents, especially early in marriage, agree on the *length* of time that you plan to stay. One idea is to allow your wife to go home to her parents a few days earlier than you in order to give her parents the attention they need before you arrive. Men, occasionally go home to see your parents alone. Sometimes parents need time alone with their children after they are married. If you live close to either parent, this will not be a problem.

Most importantly, when visiting as a couple, let your mate have the freedom to love his own parents. If you feel somewhat ignored while at your spouse's parents' home, anticipate and discuss it before your next visit.

For example, you might want to go somewhere with your wife while at her home. Since she is the one who is naturally accepted in her home, take her aside and tell her your plan. That way she can announce the need for you both to go somewhere at the appropriate time. She takes total responsibility for the decision. You are free from the possibility of hurting her parents, and they better understand and accept the decision. If in-laws tend to visit too much, agree on a plan; then the child of that in-law should talk to the parent. Don't put your mate in a position that might offend or hurt your parents. It's easier to deal with your parent yourself so your spouse is still approved and not involved in tough discussions.

Fifth, be considerate toward your in-laws. Ask your mother-in-law and father-in-law what they would prefer that you call them. Let them know you will be glad to call them Mom and Dad if they prefer. You may be more comfortable calling them by their first names, especially if you have known them for a long time. Asking gives them the freedom to say, "It's up to you."

Another thing that demonstrates consideration is dropping your parents-in-law an occasional card, thanking them for their role in your mate's life or for allowing you to visit. Courtesy with parents not only brings joy to them and to you, but increases the possibility of an exciting grandparent-child relationship in the future.

MONEY MATTERS WITH PARENTS OR IN-LAWS

A key area that can bring either gratitude or resentment is receiving financial assistance. The husband should work out a definite plan for receiving money offered by parents on either side, and then communicate that plan to both sets of parents. If a husband communicates with his father-in-law the first time that parent attempts to give the couple a gift, her father will always respect his son-in-law.

We discourage parental loans in almost every situation, but parents should have the freedom to give gifts to their children. However, a husband needs to set boundaries that ensure his authority as well as the parents' respect.

By nature, most parents are givers and children are takers. This tendency doesn't necessarily end when the child marries. Take the example of going out to dinner. Parents have always bought dinners for their children. How does a child begin to be an adult around the parent? These are the questions that need to be addressed. Who pays? When do you pay? Who invited whom?

As with most problems, communication is the key. A good rule of thumb is to address the issues before they ever come up. Every once in awhile, take your parents out to dinner. If you offer to pay, and your parents reject the offer, then you have done your part. If your parents ask you to go somewhere that is clearly beyond your means (i.e., a trip, expensive restaurant, etc.), make sure to discuss what they think is appropriate to contribute.

Because moms and dads handle money differently, they also have different expectations of their adult children. Make sure that you talk to *both* of your parents about money issues so that resentment does not develop. Remember that resentment over money issues can cause great bitterness.

Parents and parents-in-law can be a source of joy or a source of irritation. Wise is the couple who has a plan, communicates that plan (to *all* parents), and is flexible in meeting the needs of all parties. Be sure to keep your own marriage healthy. This will communicate to the parents, more than anything else, that you and your mate are one.

A WORD TO
PARENTS AND PARENTS-IN-LAW

This chapter is for couples, of course, but we have included a final section that you may want to let your parents read. Explain that the chapter on relationships with parents and in-laws has been helpful and it includes a chapter they would enjoy reading (by a couple who have been parents for thirty years and in-laws for a shorter time).

Regarding her married children, one mother said, "Lord, give me the wisdom to bite my tongue." Our hope for parents is that you trust the Lord with your children so that you won't need to bite your tongue. Let them make some mistakes (by your standards). Parents tend to give advice on how they would run things, how they would spend money, how they would raise kids, and so on. If your children don't do what they know you expect them to do, they may feel guilt.

Realize that times have changed, not scriptural values. Your children may live in nicer housing than you did at the same age. Your children may leave their children with childcare far more often than you did. Avoid developing a critical attitude. Criticism will wound your children. No one enjoys being with a critical person. Over time your children may begin to distance themselves from you, and you may destroy your opportunity to watch them grow to maturity and to enjoy them as friends.

It is wise to say to your children, "Listen to what I say, and then do as you please." This assures you of always having the freedom to offer advice and suggestions based on your experience, yet it assures your children that they can make their own decisions. This leaves the door of communication open for all of you. Allow them to then do as they please without further unsolicited advice or an "I-told-you-so" attitude.

Remember this: Criticizing your children or their spouses will only drive them away from you. If it continues, they will avoid you and will dread their times with you. Think before using the statements, "You never . . ." and "You always. . . ." Also, don't do something nice for your children, and then remind them of it. Sometimes it is best to just drop a subject than to cause conflict.

Don't forget to be sensitive to their need for privacy. If you live in close proximity, call before you visit and *don't overstay your welcome or visit too often.* Instead, establish a visiting pattern that fits everyone. Exchange visits at appropriate times. When grandchildren come, more communication will be required. Exchanged visits then become even more important. Never assume your children won't mind if you just drop over, especially early in marriage. When both husband and wife work, their time in the evenings and on weekends may be their only time for privacy. Be as considerate of them as you would your other friends.

Make sure your daughter-in-law or son-in-law feels welcome in your home and with your family. Balance your gifts equally to your married children and their spouses. Treat them as part of the family and they will be. If you do, God will use you in their lives in ways you would never dream. This may be their first opportunity to observe mature Christian parents. Fathers, initiate time with your son-in-law so the daughter can spend time with her mom.

Finally, many couples today have several sets of in-laws if their parents have been divorced. This obviously can cause problems, especially around the holidays. If this is the case with you, allow your children and spouses to visit all the parents involved.

With sensitivity and love, you can become a source of joy to your children all the days of your lives.

SIXTEEN

God's
Testing Times

$\mathcal{I}$ remember when I (Don) first began to understand the biblical importance of trials as a new Christian. My initial assumption was that successful Christians missed the most trials, similar to running through a minefield and dodging the mines. Years of study, counseling, and personal experience have changed my perspective. I've hit a few of those mines, and you probably have also. Indeed, many of the trials we face in marriage are universal. Therefore, we should identify them and be prepared to deal with them.

Here is God's perspective on trials: "For you have been called for this purpose, since Christ also suffered for you, leaving you an example for you to follow in His steps" (1 Peter 2:21).

At first, I could not imagine that it was actually part of God's plan for me to experience trials. But the more I thought about the above verse and its message, the more it made sense. If I had been called to salvation by Jesus Christ and given His inheritance, it seemed reasonable that I would be called to share in His suffering also.

The same is true with our marriages. Without trials we probably would not depend on the Lord very often. As husbands and wives, our human natures are bent toward lustful desires and self-centeredness. In His grace, God reminds us through trials of our need for Him in the marriage. Trials humble us and cause us to depend on God. When a husband is humbled, he tends to notice his spouse instead of himself. Similarly, a wife facing trials, tough as they are, finds they are redemptive in her life. Often the only anchor a husband and wife have during a trial is the reality of Christ and His Word.

GOD'S PURPOSE IN TRIALS

God's purpose for allowing trials in your life and marriage is revealed in James 1:2–4: "Consider it all joy, my brethren, when you encounter various trials, knowing that the testing of your faith produces endurance. And let endurance have its perfect result, so that you may be perfect and complete, lacking in nothing." Several things stand out in this passage. First, James says *when,* not if, you encounter trials. As a Christian, you will definitely encounter trials. They are not an option. Further, these trials will result from a variety of sources. The word various comes from a Greek word that means "multicolored." Trials come in many hues and from different sources.

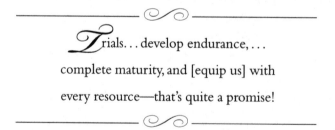

*T*rials . . . develop endurance, . . .

complete maturity, and [equip us] with

every resource—that's quite a promise!

In a world where unfulfilled marriages are robbing people of their best hope in relationships, having endurance is no small thing. God promises that the result of endurance will be that you may be "perfect and complete, lacking in nothing." Trials not only develop endurance but maturity. The phrase "lacking in nothing" means equipped with every resource. Endurance, complete maturity, and being equipped with every resource—that's quite a promise!

Maintaining a joyful spirit when either you or your mate is experiencing a trial is not a natural human response, but a faith-oriented response. Christ suffered because He knew that by going to the Cross you and I would someday be with Him in eternity. "For the 'joy' set before Him [He] endured the cross, despising the shame" (Hebrews 12:2). He looked beyond the suffering of the Cross to those of us who would spend eternity with Him. When it comes to trials, we must do the same thing—look beyond the suffering.

James also indicates that God will approve the person who perseveres. "Blessed is a man who perseveres under trial; for once he has been approved, he will receive the crown of life which the Lord has promised to those who love Him" (James 1:12). The word *blessed* refers to the very highest experience; in this case, God's approval. "Approved" was the word stamped on cookware after it came out of the potter's fire with no cracks. God may sometimes turn up the heat to remove the cracks in your life. After being tested, each person is promised a stamp of approval.

With a thought of joy and expectation, look at some of the trials you may suffer in marriage. Don't be caught off guard by trials when they come. When shocked by trials, you may have a tendency to blame others. Often couples go through trials and blame their mates for what God is allowing to happen in their lives.

OUR PERSONAL "THORNS IN THE FLESH"

Almost every person has one or two areas in his or her life that are just plain tough. Paul mentioned one such problem in 2 Corinthians 12. In order to limit his pride, God gave him a "thorn in the flesh" (verse 7) to keep him from exalting himself. We cannot be sure what Paul's problem was, but he clearly called it a weakness.

> Concerning this I implored the Lord three times that it might leave me. And He has said to me, "My grace is sufficient for you, for power is perfected in weakness." Most gladly, therefore, I will rather boast about my weaknesses, so that the power of Christ may dwell in me. Therefore, I am well content with weaknesses, with insults, with distresses, with persecutions, with difficulties, for Christ's sake; for when I am weak, then I am strong. (verses 8–10)

Many people have burdens to bear. Your acceptance of the thorns you have is vital to maturing in your Christian life. You can prepare yourself for the possibility that you and your mate will have at least one area that will probably never change and you will have to view it as Paul did his thorn.

For some people it might be stubbornness, a weight problem, temper, sloppiness, or low self-image. I have seen some great men with pride problems and some with insecurities. In my own life, my insecurity related to public speaking is definitely a problem, my "thorn in the flesh." I am convinced that it is there for my good and that it will become a source of strength in my life. Public speaking is an area I have fought, questioned, and agonized with God about; it has caused my family some trauma, and me some heartache, yet it is still there.

In working through my thorn, I have been able to recognize other peoples' thorns. I know there are millions of marriages where mates are paralyzed because of some unchangeable weakness in themselves or their mates that has robbed them of all hope and joy.

If you or your mate have a problem that seems impossible to work with, approach it as Paul did. If it never changes, then thank God for it and ask Him to use it in your life to develop endurance, patience, maturity, and compassion.

VARIOUS TRIALS:
Our Jobs, Children, and Relationships

We will face many trials as married adults. Many of the tensions, arguments, and heartaches are caused by the transgression or misunderstanding of others. But often the trial comes through our own personal sins or irresponsible behavior. In this section, we will consider how to respond to our own sins and those of others.

If you determine that you brought the trial into your life through sin or a bad decision, confess it to God. After confessing, begin to take the appropriate steps to resolve it. Be sure to seek forgiveness from others when appropriate.

The following three areas are examples of trials people create—problems resulting from unresolved broken relationships with friends, family, and children, financial irresponsibility, jealousy, gossip, and uncontrolled anger.

Concerning trials on our jobs, let's recognize first that as career men and women move through life, they go through many cycles in their working relationships. Everyone needs to work hard and feel both productive and appreciated. There are a number of factors that affect a person's happiness at work, such as knowing he or she is in the right job, being excited about going to work, enjoying his or her work, and being proud of the job done.

Men and women—including wives and mothers, who as home-makers have tasks that can give both satisfaction and benefit others—need to prepare for trials in their work. You may be happy one day and dissatisfied the next. Wives need to trust and support their husbands during periods of dissatisfaction, which can last for extended lengths of time. Husbands, likewise, need to understand and encourage their wives who work in the home or in an outside job.

Job frustration is a normal and predictable problem in life. One of the main sources of stress while working outside the home is fellow workers. Jealous supervisors, insensitive owners, coworkers who gossip, and those with irritating personalities are not unusual. Their negative actions, like ours, are caused by sinful, selfish natures, yet we cannot ignore them. At times, going to work is painful.

Here are some suggestions to deal with trials in the workplace. First, identify these incidents as trials. Then talk to your mate about them. An understanding and supportive mate will strengthen you at such times. Pull together! Support each other while developing a plan to correct the problems (where it's in your power to do so). Seek counsel if you need to.

Working men and women can become accountable to several older adults of the same sex, preferably in their church, to help them evaluate and keep perspective during trials. For women working as homemakers, both husbands and older, mature Christian women can provide support for the daily tensions of maintaining the home.

Continually evaluate if you are doing what you enjoy and do well. If not, consider contacting an agency for counsel and a career assessment. We recommend Life Pathways, a division of Christian Financial Concepts. Life Pathways can help you to develop a conservative strategy and to move slowly toward what you enjoy and do well.

Concerning the rearing of children, we believe that children are a major blessing in life, yet realize they can also be a source of major trials along the way. They, like us, are sinners, and we are rearing them to become independent adults. That means they will make mistakes and disappoint us. We need to be patient and forgiving of them. It also means we will make mistakes as we correct and help them. During the child-rearing years, the trials will come regularly.

Men, if you support your wife in these trials, you will make these times much easier and a greater blessing for your family. A woman's major mission field is often her children. She will tend to evaluate her worth in life in terms of her children's success. It is not a surprise, then, that God would use children to teach women dependence. If husbands share this responsibility properly, wives will feel less stress.

The initial trials with children can develop as early as during pregnancy and the first year of a child's life, for the newborn and un-born are indeed needy. An understanding and patient husband will help with meals and housework both during pregnancy and the first months of the baby's life. Though some trials are momentary and passing, babies can disrupt a mother with their sickness, sleeping problems, and scheduling. The husband must be able to help his wife during these times, and not allow her to take all of the responsibility.

When children reach school age, parents begin to observe poten-tial emotional, intellectual, and spiritual needs. Anticipate these trials and support one another. Fathers, stay involved in your children's ac-complishments, failures, and disappointments. Don't let those failures and disappointments—including those that are actually based on your own expectations or preferences—make you upset; instead, encour-age your children. And don't leave school discipline problems to your wife. Instead, plan to visit your child's teacher with your wife.

The process of disciplining children is a continual trial, especially for mothers. Husbands can save their wives much frustration by tak-ing responsibility for part of the discipline. We recommend that the father take a three-day period every two months to run a discipline check and then fine-tune his children's discipline. Children respond beautifully to fathers who take authority and spend quality time with them. A father who disciplines but fails to spend time loving his children makes a serious mistake. It takes both love and discipline to develop healthy relationships.

Concerning personal relationships, realize that as husband and wife, each of you will face challenges and disappointments with friends and acquaintances on the job, in the neighborhood, and at church. How you deal with hurtful relationships as a couple will largely determine your happiness in life. Why? Dealing with hurt quickly can prevent anger and bitterness from developing. Not dealing with such tensions can lead to the bitterness that robs couples of hope and faith.

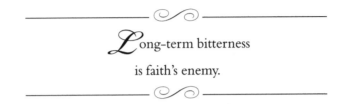

Long-term bitterness

is faith's enemy.

Prepare for trials in working relationships. Realize that people will fail to appreciate you, use you for selfish purposes, blame you for failure, question your abilities, and even cut you out of future plans. These typical hurts can cause bitterness. Gear up for these occasional shocks and protect your spouse when he or she encounters such trials. Losing a job or missing a promotion is a small thing for the Lord to overcome. Remember: Long-term bitterness is faith's enemy. Help one another to maintain hope in the Lord and His Word during these trials. Also remember that *people are not your enemies.* Satan wants you to believe that they are in order to distract and discourage you.

Church relationships, close friends, family, and neighbors are sources of potential trials. Aggressively apply the law of love, but expect occasional hurts. When it happens, renew your mind, and pull together as a couple. Above all, don't be critical of others.

TRIALS OF GREAT PAIN:
Death of Family Member, Infertility, Divorce

Many couples face trials that produce great pain, including the death of a family member, infertility, and divorce.

Whether it be a parent, child, or friend, eventually you will lose a family member. Christ removed the sting of death, yet we still suffer the loss here on Earth. *Death* can be very discouraging and depressing. Husbands and wives must stand together in their pain, pray for one another, and seek help when necessary.

Losing a child is one of the most painful and devastating trials in life. The pain often lasts years, and only God can bring you through it with hope and healing. As Christians, our view of death is different than the world's perspective. God also gives us other people to offer comfort, and we can welcome them. Others who have experienced this loss can become valuable allies in time of need. Support groups are very important as well.

A husband . . . must convince her that

his love is not contingent upon her ability

to conceive and bear children.

And, as you receive comfort, remember God gives you a great opportunity to give back to others: "[God] comforts us in all our troubles, so that we can comfort those in any trouble with the comfort we ourselves have received from God. For just as the sufferings of Christ flow over into our lives, so also through Christ our comfort overflows" (2 Corinthians 1:4–5 NIV).

Infertility may be more common than you think. Even if you never personally face infertility, it is likely you will meet someone who will. The number of couples having difficulties conceiving children has increased significantly in recent years, though the reasons for the dramatic climb have remained unclear. New research seems to point to longer use of the birth control pill and pregnancy in later years as the largest factors causing infertility. Past abortions may also have a negative effect. The latest statistic is that one in six couples has difficulty getting pregnant. Some cannot get pregnant without medical help.

The emotional and financial toll caused by this problem can be hurtful, as well as discouraging. A husband may expect his wife to feel like a failure. He must convince her that his love is not contingent upon her ability to conceive and bear children. Remind her from Scripture that God not only makes rich and poor, but He also controls the womb. Help turn her perspective to God by reminding her that she is your provision from the Lord, with or without children. A wife needs to emotionally support her husband who may be the reason for the infertility. He can blame himself for the inability of his wife to conceive, also.

There are many doctors today who specialize in fertility. Good support groups exist to help couples confront this potentially painful situation, and they can give much guidance and comfort. Couples who face this trial should seek God's perspective on each possible solution.

His perspective will give comfort. For instance, many infertile couples feel that they are being judged by God for some past sins. Although infertility was a temporal curse under the Mosaic Law (see, for example, Leviticus 26:9, 15; Deuteronomy 28:4, 11, 18), those warnings are part of the Old Covenant God had with the children of Israel. We cannot apply the Old Covenant to God's relationship with us in the New Covenant. To do so is to misuse the Scriptures.

Properly applying the Scriptures can actually give infertile couples hope for one loving remedy: adoption. Adoption is used as one of the most significant descriptions of our relationship with God in the New Covenant. When we trust Christ as our personal Savior, God "adopts" us as His own children forever, according to the Scriptures. (See Romans 8:15, 23; Galatians 4:4–6; and Ephesians 1:5–6.) Since God has adopted us into His forever family, we can consider human adoption as a divine alternative to infertility. What a divine blessing to be able to love and disciple children who would not otherwise come in contact with the things of God. Adoption can be very fulfilling for those who sense in prayer that God is directing them into this joyful adventure. If you choose to adopt, remember that adopted children, like biological children, will bring challenges that require love, patience, and understanding.

Finally, *divorce* represents one of the most painful periods of any person's life, hurting both spouses and any children. If you are considering divorce, we urge you to view that as a last resort. Get counsel, read the Scriptures, and see if the marriage can be healed.

If divorce (or separation) has already occurred, seek God's wisdom in His Word and from godly mentors and counselors. Those who have undergone divorce often feel they're failures and unworthy; sometimes they are unable to trust anyone afterward. The divorced must deal with grief and release anger and bitterness. It's OK to grieve and be angry for a season, but don't stay there and become bitter. The divorced also must learn to forgive and often need to reestablish their faith in God. With forgiveness comes healing of the soul and mind.

During such crisis points, solace comes ultimately in God—seeking His face through Bible study, prayer, and sometimes fasting. If you are contemplating remarriage, be sure you have come to the point of once more trusting God and trusting others. Forgiveness reestablishes faith, and faith causes us to mature, in spite of deep pain in our lives.

When it comes to any trial, if you have not brought the trial into your life, assume it is from God's loving hand for your benefit and His glory. Begin to apply the perspectives taught in Scripture concerning trials. Thank the Lord for each trial and you will be blessed for your faith.

TRIALS OF THE EVERYDAY

Often our trials are not the heartache of death, the absence of children, or the pain of fractured relationships. There are the trials of the everyday living as husband and wife. Two trials you should be alert to as a family are the pressures of moving and busy schedules.

America is such a mobile society that people change residences frequently. Yet few things affect the emotional security of a family more. Selling your home and buying another one, followed by the move, are only the beginning. Many other things change: relationships, church and organizational ties, friends, and security. New frontiers must be forged, new relationships built, a new job begun, and a new church home established. Probably the most difficult part of a move is making new friends. It takes several years to replace good friends.

Your children also experience tremendous loss, especially their close friends. Be very patient and tender with them as they go through their tears and ask "why?"

Since moving is so common, it is important as a couple to support one another in all the changes. Begin by making the decision together; include the whole family when possible, and then work out a total plan that gives everyone hope. God doesn't often move people into a spiritual vacuum. Before you finalize your move, also try to find a church home.

You need time for yourself, for romance,
for the children, for ministry, for hobbies.

Pray about everything as you plan the move. Years ago, before our move from Dallas to Little Rock, we prayed for specific things. Todd prayed for a creek in the backyard, Carmen prayed for a two-story house, and Sally prayed for red brick with yellow trim. We flew to Little Rock, found a realtor, and told her what we wanted. She said, "I've got just the house." And it was. We also prayed for a neighborhood with children, friends for Sally, and a church like the one in Dallas. We ended up starting a church just like the one in Dallas. God specifically answered all of these requests. We had not prayed specifically for our previous moves, and for the most part, those moves were more anguishing. I am convinced that if we spend time on our knees, God will know our requests! He will glorify Himself by meeting our needs as a family.

And what about busy family schedules? Managing time usually becomes one of the biggest trials in married life. You need time for yourself, for romance, for the children, for ministry, for hobbies—even time just to read a good book. Many Christians trying to do what is right in their marriages usually lose the battle with their schedules.

You must get tough with establishing priorities. There are so many responsibilities and good things to distract you that only a clear commitment to time priority will suffice.

Men, take responsibility here. A wife cannot do much without her husband's involvement. First, decide on your major priorities, listing what you need to accomplish in each area. After that, you will have to eliminate almost everything else. Sally and I discuss our schedules in order to gain input and suggestions from each other. Just communicating helps us to eliminate unneeded or unwanted things in our schedules. We have learned that trials result from becoming overcommitted. Husbands and wives can help each other say, "No, I can't do that right now." Those are difficult words to say, but it helps if we understand our limitations.

Because of the importance of time control and schedule in relation to a man's priorities, I occasionally will ask two or three close Christian brothers to sit down and go over my schedule. After Sally gives her perspective, I try to schedule a meeting with these men six weeks later to evaluate my schedule and priorities. Sally also makes herself accountable with other women. If they agree with us on our busy schedules, then we know it is momentarily workable and our priorities are in the order the Lord would desire.

For accountability, husbands should consider joining a men's accountability group. Because men usually have difficulty expressing feelings, hurt, frustration, and struggles, a group creates accountability in these areas. For women, small prayer groups or Bible studies are invaluable for friendships, as well as accountability and encouragement. Couples would do well to learn to be leaders of small groups within their churches. These small groups could include marriage studies, parenting issues, the Christian faith, and financial studies.

FINDING VISION THROUGH OUR TRIALS

Often the very trial you go through may in fact be saving your life and may eventually save someone else's. Our ministry organization, Christian Family Life, and this book were the result of trials we encountered in early marriage. Many organizations and support groups, such as Mothers Against Drunk Driving and Alcoholics Anonymous, started because of painful trials in someone's life. Almost all biblical characters endured various trials. So you are not alone. The very trial that you may be experiencing now may, in fact, lead you to your life's work. Life, at best, brings uncertainty and trials, but these trials are always good for us. They teach us contentment in life and dependence on God. As the apostle Paul wrote:

Not that I speak from want; for I have learned to be content in whatever circumstances I am. I know how to get along with humble means, and I also know how to live in prosperity; in any and every circumstance I have learned the secret of being filled and going hungry, both of having abundance and suffering need. I can do all things through Him who strengthens me. (Philippians 4:11–13)

The better you are at anticipating trials, the more growth you will experience in your faith. The greater your faith, the greater your spiritual maturity. There is a difference in anticipating trials and living in worry and anxiety. Look beyond the trial and ask God how He wants to use it. God is good, and He has a purpose for every trial that we encounter.

Epilogue

In chapter 1 we recounted how the two of us experienced a turbulent beginning to marriage, like many couples. Our struggle provoked this question, "If God designed marriage, can He make it work?" We found the answer to be a resounding yes. We trust this book has led you to the same answer.

Our central message declares that spiritual marriages require faith. When speaking of Scripture's greatest examples of faith, the writer of Hebrews said, "And without faith it is impossible to please Him, for he who comes to God must believe that He is and that He is a rewarder of those who seek Him" (Hebrews 11:6). Faith demonstrates our belief in God and, as a result, pleases Him. It is no surprise that God designed marriage to increase our faith in Him. We cannot please Him without faith.

Faith requires two things. First, it requires that we know and trust Him as God, the creator of heaven and earth. Second, if we truly know Him, we are to trust Him to reward us according to His magnificent promises. No individual can love by faith without believing that God's Word is more powerful than their mate's weaknesses.

True faith always produces good works. As your faith produces good works toward your mate, God will astonish you by fulfilling His magnificent promises to you from His Word. Faith allows us to override our natural selfishness by choosing to act on God's Word. Faith then releases God to do what He said He would do.

To experience a supernatural "faith marriage," your spouse and you must embrace each of the commitments discussed in this book. Let's quickly review these commitments:

1. Each of you must openly confess your selfish tendencies. Commit to change the course of your marriage in the future by seeking a faith relationship.

2. Each of you must accept your responsibility from God to fulfill His purposes of *reflecting* God's image, *reproducing* His image through children and disciples, and *reigning* on earth to His glory. These purposes require oneness between husband and wife.

3. Each of you must accept from God that you were created with a relational need that can be met only by God. Then, by faith, you must receive your mate as God's personal provision for your aloneness need.

4. Loving your mate by faith will require you to individually submit your will to the Holy Spirit's ministry in your life. This means you must allow the Holy Spirit to convict, teach, lead, and empower you. Remember, marital oneness cannot exist apart from the Holy Spirit.

5. Marital oneness requires each of you to understand God's agents for change in marriage. Scripture endorses two forces of change: (1) sacrificial love as demonstrated by Christ and (2) returning a blessing when wronged. You must trust God to change your mate as you faithfully love and bless him or her.

6. The divine order of oneness is love and submission, as illustrated in the Trinity of God (1 Corinthians 11:3 and John 17:20–21).

It takes great faith, spiritual insight, and trust to joyfully love and submit. Each of you must ask God for wisdom on a daily basis to defeat Satan's worldly deceit.

7. Displaying godly traits toward each other requires your being people of faith. Such traits will bring harmony and peace to your home.

These commitments form the basis of a supernatural faith relationship. Good intentions or natural desires will never result in a faith relationship. A faith relationship results from knowing and applying God's Word. How do you know if you have a faith relationship? The only way to know is for both mates to commit to the above insights by faith. Sally and I, as good as our original intentions were, did not understand these insights when we married. Later we understood and committed to these principles, and our marriage changed dramatically.

Such faith commitments will affect the practical areas of marriage, including sex, finances, and communication. Each of you must discover what God's Word says on each subject and then apply it by faith.

It takes time and effort to fully discover a supernatural faith relationship. But make no mistake—a faith relationship starts by understanding and applying the six insights just summarized. Do not put this book down until you have made these commitments by faith. Then share them with others to deepen and revitalize your understanding over time.

In 1979, when we first wrote this book (having been married only twelve years), Sally and I experienced firsthand the results of God's principles of marriage in our own lives. Now, twenty-plus years later, we have been more than pleased to still experience joy in each other, to laugh and play together, to work together, to write and create together. But most rewarding is the fact that all four of our children are walking with God. As we have tried to reflect God's image as a couple and reign together as a couple, God has rewarded us with a godly heritage.

Three of our children have married spouses who love and walk with God. We have been blessed also with all three of their spouses' godly families. What rich rewards! We say all of this not because our kids have been perfect but because God said if we obey Him, He would bless us. And bless us He has! We say this to give the honor where honor is due: to God the Father, God the Son, and God the Holy Spirit.

Sally and I pray that you too will be able to apply the following verses to your marriage: "For this reason a man shall leave his father and his mother, and be joined to his wife; and they shall become one flesh. And the man and his wife were both naked and were not ashamed" (Genesis 2:24–25). We wish each of you the joy of being totally exposed to each other with no fear or threat. If you miss this joy of being one, you will have missed much of God's blessing on this earth. Only faith can release God's blessing in your marriage.

OTHER RESOURCES
FROM CHRISTIAN FAMILY LIFE

Don and Sally Meredith founded Christian Family Life, Inc., in 1971 to further the training of professional counselors as well as laypeople. In 1976, they helped start the Family Life Ministry of Campus Crusade for Christ. The Merediths, who are marriage counselors, developed a discipleship course designed for married and engaged couples.

The course is contained in the *Two . . .Becoming One Workbook.* The workbook helps couples to implement the principles from *Two . . . Becoming One* into their lives. We encourage you to consider the workbook as a follow-up tool for applying the principles of this book and enriching your marriage. The book, the workbook, and a leader's guide are available from your local Christian bookstore. (All are published by Moody Press.) If you are not near a Christian bookstore, you may order through us at 888-875-0578.

You may want to consider promoting or leading a church or at-home class to study the workbook. If you would like more information on organizing or leading such a group study, we invite you to write or call: Christian Family Life, Inc., 5301 W.T. Harris Boulevard, Charlotte, NC, 28269, 704-596-9630. Our E-mail address is Chfamily@ratedg.com, and our FAX number is 704-596-4255.